LIVING GOD'S LOVE

DOUGLAS COOPER

Pacific Press Publishing Association
Boise, Idaho
Montemorelos, Nuevo Leon, Mexico
Oshawa, Ontario, Canada

Design by Lauren Smith

Library of Congress Catalog Card No. 74-27171

ISBN 0-8163-0176-X

85 86 87 88 89 90 ● 12 11 10 9 8

CONTENTS

THE IMPERATIVE OF LOVING WELL

"The spirit of man is the candle of the Lord." Proverbs 20:27.

From a distance, the California State Prison for drug addicts still has the appearance of the fabulous resort hotel it used to be. Secluded among the rolling hills near the small town of Corona, it was a place of retreat for the Hollywood set at one time. Then the depression hit. Business dropped off, and the anxious owners sold to the state.

The pleasant little blue-green lake, circled with leafy shade trees in the middle of the grounds, still lends a relaxed atmosphere. The uniformed guards, the tightly-strung barbed wire, and the imposing iron gates quickly force the realization, however, that not all the occupants are there because they want to be.

As our group stepped in line to begin a tour of the institution, a guard firmly pressed an invisible stamp on the inside of each of our wrists. It would be necessary, we were told, to pass that marked spot under a special ultraviolet light in order to facilitate regaining our freedom later in the day. This gave final credence to the fact that we were going into a prison.

5

The hours slid by rapidly as we were escorted into different areas and given explanations of philosophies and facilities of rehabilitation. After a time the authorities invited our group to join some of the inmates for an informal talk session.

There I met Jim. He stood out. A tall handsome man of about forty with his hair turning steel gray at the temples, he seemed to have a special quality about him.

As the discussion got under way, I noticed that he remained silent while many of the other prisoners spoke out freely about themselves and their problems.

Jim did not say anything until he learned through the conversation that some in our group of visitors were ministers.

When he cleared his throat quietly, the others stopped talking.

Speaking softly, he began, "I want to share something with you fellows. Maybe it will help.

"I am a medical doctor. I had a real going practice back home. I had a beautiful and faithful wife. Two fine sons. I had the respect and confidence of the people in my community. More and more patients came to my office all the time. My surgery schedule grew heavier and heavier. My rounds at the hospital began to take longer and longer. Soon I didn't even have time for half a day off a week. I began running way behind on sleep. It seemed like there was an emergency or a delivery every night.

"Finally, out of desperation, I began taking drugs to give me a little extra lift. Oh, I didn't use much at first, just enough to keep me going during the rough spots of the day. It didn't even bother me at first. I was certain that I could control myself.

"But then it happened. Before I was really aware, I was hooked. I couldn't stop and stay together. I knew I would go completely to pieces if I got off. If that happened, I knew it would be the end of everything.

"Believe it or not, I did not know what to do or where to turn. I did recognize that I needed help desperately. I felt that I could not trust any other doctor. I was afraid it would not be kept quiet, and I would lose my license."

Jim paused and stared at his hands as he talked to us. There was complete, unbroken, silence in the room for a few seconds. Then he continued.

"Well, I had been brought up a church member. I had even attended church after becoming a physician, when I had the time.

"I decided there was only one man I could turn to with my problem. That was my minister. I would go to him. I had hope that he would understand. Most of all, I think I wanted someone who would help me get in touch with God. I think I knew even then that this was the only way out for me.

"I made an appointment with my pastor one day and went to his office. I was desperate by then. I didn't waste any time. I told him that I was taking drugs. I told him that I knew I was actually an addict and that I couldn't seem to find a way to get myself out of the chaotic mess I was in.

"I suppose I was too direct," Jim said. "I will never forget his reaction. He looked at me in utter horror and amazement. He blurted out, 'Oh! My God! No, Jim! Not you!'

"Then he began to lecture me about what a terrible

thing I was doing to my family and to the church. He went into detail about the effect it was going to have on my practice and my reputation. He ended up by reminding me that such an awful mistake would undoubtedly lead to the destruction of my soul in hell."

Again Jim stopped. When he began to speak again, it was even more softly and thoughtfully than before.

"I have never felt so disappointed, so let down, so alone in all of my life. I had gone to the man in a desperate search for someone to listen to me. For someone to talk to. For someone to help me.

"I already knew that what I was doing was bad. I already knew that it was wrong and sinful for me to be involved as I was. I already knew that I should stop. That is why I went to him in the first place. I didn't need any reminders about what I already knew.

"I suppose that it was partly because of my discouragement and disappointment over what happened that day that I lost all hope of pulling out of the downward spiral I was in and ended up here. Please don't misunderstand. I am not trying to put the blame on anyone else but myself. I am the one that blew my own life. I have learned a great deal about life and about myself since I have been here. And so many times I just wish so much that many things could have been different. Maybe I could have made it."

Then, with all the hurt and pain and frustration that came to him that day he had gone to seek help from his pastor still very real to him, the prisoner looked directly at us and said, "So I just want to tell you fellows something. Please, if an addict or someone else who really needs help with something ever comes to you, don't lecture him. Just listen to him and love him as he is. Maybe then you can help him."

A failure at loving, though it often goes unrecognized, is always tragic. Why? *Because at the heart of Christianity is a God of love, who wishes to reveal that love through one person to another.* When callousness, indifference, prejudice, or a host of other possible barriers get in the way, *God's divine purpose is thwarted.* For this to happen even once is too much.

Since the Father's plan for reaching the hearts of needy, sinful, dying men is based on using His children to share His love in the world, the gospel in its most dynamic form consists of loving people well. Loving them where they are and as they are. This is pure evangelism at its best.

A failure at loving is serious because it jeopardizes someone's eternal life. It may cut off what would have been God's opportunity to draw a man to Him at a time when the man needs Him the most.

That is what happened to Jim.

It is a fact that, to begin with anyway, most people cannot understand or experience the love of God apart from other men. It has to be reflected to them from the mirror of another life before it becomes real to them and before they can respond to it.

For reasons unfathomable to us, the Father has chosen to make Himself vulnerable to His own by allowing Himself to depend on us to provide a demonstration in human terms today of what He is and what His love is.

"The spirit of man," the Bible says, "is the candle of the Lord." Proverbs 20:27. Thus, through His people,

9

the Father desires to light the world with His love.

Can you see, then, why it is such a very serious thing when one of us fails at loving another person well? It may cause the very credibility of the existence of God and the love of God to be diminished for that other individual.

In his book *Happiness Wall to Wall* George Vandeman points out dramatically that divorce, the all-too-common breakdown and failure of a human love relationship, is tragic because God "wanted to use your love, father and mother, to explain His own love to a child. And now He can't!" Page 34.

I remember trying to counsel a fourteen-year-old boy. A problem student at the church school—sullen, uncommunicative, uncooperative. No one seemed to be able to get through to him.

He had been abandoned by his father after his mother died. The early years of his life were spent in an orphanage. More recently he had been shifted from one foster home to another. Finally he had come to live with some church people, who in spite of their experience and patience with children, were ready to give up on trying to keep this unfortunate youth.

I talked to the lad one day in a little cramped library room where the school principal had sent him to see me.

I can still hear myself telling him how his heavenly Father loved him.

I marvel now that he did not laugh outright at me. I deserved it.

You see, to someone who has never known the love of an earthly father or mother, it is an extremely difficult thing to comprehend a loving heavenly Father.

Countless emotional barriers exist which dramatically impair spiritual reality. How can they believe that God, whom they cannot see, loves them, when even people whom they can see have never loved them in any significant way? At least not when it would have counted most.

Almost always, anyone who is at such an emotional and spiritual disadvantage has to experience deeply the warmth of genuine human love before they can or will ever respond to the love of God.

Our world today is full of the insecure, the unloved. In the United States about one out of three marriages ends in divorce. And most of the rest are often unhappy. Hosts of empty lives result as the chief God-ordained structure of human love disintegrates. This makes it increasingly difficult for men to be open to experiencing God and His love.

Guilt, fear, and deep anxiety are increasing. The cancers of hatred, rebellion, dissatisfaction, disillusionment, and violence proliferate daily. Evil has taken on a keen aggressiveness, a dramatic boldness.

The most drastic results cannot be seen on the surface. The effects go far deeper than just the wrong acts done, the laws broken, the morals ruined, the disrespect shown.

It is not the ethics of the sin explosion that should cause the greatest concern to Christians!

Something far worse about it is eating out the heart of the unfortunate inhabitants of planet Earth. The Bible speaks concisely of a greater tragedy associated with the overwhelming increase of wickedness that will just precede the second coming of Jesus Christ. "And

11

because iniquity shall abound, the love of many shall wax cold." Matthew 24:12.

The Christian's primary task today is not to bemoan and lament over the increasing tide of evil on every hand. Of itself this accomplishes no great good. Rather, the challenge is to get on with the supreme task of bringing the gospel, which is the good news about a God of love, to a generation that does not know what love is because the exploding force of wickedness has practically wiped it out of human lives.

We desperately need to have a love, given us by Jesus, to share in this world that will meet and match the abounding wickedness of the day. In this final hour we must help people experience this sort of love through us—in depth. We cannot, we must not fail at loving people—well.

To help us all, under God, to meet this ultimate of challenges, this book is dedicated.

2

THE GREATEST SIN

"We have turned every one to his own way."
Isaiah 53:6.

It was to have been her first child. The room that had been reserved so long for "baby" had been scrubbed and the floor polished. Pictures of dancing ponies and cuddly puppies now decorated the walls.

The new bassinet had come in for its share of attention too. It stood regally in the center of the room. Its supporting legs were covered by a flowing curtain of white silk trimmed with delicate lace. Inside, on top of the fluffy yellow blanket, two pairs of carefully hand-knitted booties waited. One pair was pink. The other blue.

When the pain first came, it was exciting to experience the birth process begin to happen. But by the time she had been admitted to the hospital, she sensed something wrong.

The doctor came. He took her hand, a hand now white-pale, blue veins standing out clearly under the skin. He held it quietly for a moment in a rather professional way, expressing concern and compassion. He told her that severe complications had occurred.

Surgery was going to be necessary immediately. As kindly as he could he explained that the surgery was necessary to save her life. It was too late to save the child.

The doctor, a Christian physician, later told of the crushing effect this news had on the young woman. In her anguish and despair she requested her minister and husband. There were also certain rites to be performed at such a time according to the teachings of her church. Being a faithful member, she was deeply concerned that they be administered.

The doctor phoned the clergyman at once and explained what had happened and asked him to come quickly. The man on the other end of the line replied that he was busy at the moment with something else. He said that it would be more convenient for him if he could drop by the hospital the next day when he had more time. He added that under the circumstances the doctor himself, or a nurse, could perform the practical steps that would satisfy the administering of the necessary rites to the child. With that he hung up.

To many, sin is not believing what should be believed. Or not obeying what should be obeyed. They think of it as consisting only of transgressing the Ten Commandments. To limit a concept of sin, however, does not even approach an adequate understanding. It fails in understanding its true heinousness.

There is a text in Isaiah which states, "All we like sheep have gone astray." Isaiah 53:6. It is commonly and correctly interpreted to mean that every single person is a sinner. What is fascinating about this text is that the writer does not stop with the one basic, inspired observation. He continues on to give the Bible's most candid definition of sin. He adds simply, "we have turned every one to his own way."

That is what sin is all about! It is putting one's own self first, and God and others second. It is walking in our own way, no matter how "right" or "proper" or "moral" that way might be of itself, while God's way for us we reject or ignore.

According to the Master Himself, God's way, the heart of Christianity is loving the Father and loving people with all our heart and soul and body. It can only follow that *the opposite of Christianity, and therefore the essence of sin, is failing to love.*

In plainest human terms, sin is failing to love by being primarily interested in meeting one's own needs while ignoring the needs of other human beings. This is turning to our own way. This is precisely what the clergyman did when he would not go to the hospital that day to be with the young woman who was asking for him in her hour of great need.

The world and the church are full of those who are failing God and people this way. Most do not even realize the utter sinfulness of their self-centered life-style. A vast majority of even professedly Christian people today are so fervently bound up, so passionately conditioned to meet their own needs only, so totally enveloped in the confining cocoon of their own selfishness, that no one else's needs really matter.

A government operated by men who are this way will eventually ruin even the strongest nation.

Business organizations managed by people who do not care about the best good of others, but which exist

15

only to further their own interests, will in time corrupt all of society.

A church with members who routinely choose to ignore the needs of people, no matter how correct its theology, serves neither God nor man. Many sincere efforts to communicate the gospel often lack a vitally needed element. Instead of the torch being passed, it is so often fumbled. The fire of love has almost gone out.

The experience of the Ephesus church is an example. Their first service for God caused their Lord to delight in the light of heaven reflected by revealing the spirit of Christ in tenderness and compassion.

Unfortunately the time came when they neglected to hold dear the supremacy of love. Substitute priorities took its place. Self got in the way. The emphasis shifted, and the Christians at Ephesus began to fail at their primary responsibility of revealing the love of God to the world. They neglected to pass on Christ's compassion and tenderness. They eventually lost that which had once been *everything* to them.

The flame had gone out.

Down through history the Christian church has repeated this tragedy again and again. And there is the clear-cut warning that the final church, the Laodicean church, will make the same awful mistake. It will come to the place where its greatest need will be for a real, practical experience in the love of God. The True Witness will be forced to give the counsel that its only hope lies in seeking diligently the "gold tried in the fire." The gold of love.

This church is a prosperous church—"rich, and increased with goods." It is successful. It is capable.

Self-sufficient. It has everything. Needs nothing—except love.

"The condition of many of those who claim to be the children of God is exactly represented by the message to the Laodicean church," Christian writer Ellen G. White once wrote. "Those who have a knowledge of the truth do not understand it as fully as they might. *They do not bring the love of Christ into the heart and life.*"

The church today has expert ministers whose eloquence and ability combine perfectly to do a splendid job of communicating truth and encouraging belief.

The church has expert administrators—people whose talent for giving management and direction may be on a par with that of the finest corporate executives.

The church has public relations experts—people carefully schooled in the techniques of projecting the right image of the organization to the public.

The church has financial experts—individuals whose keen knowledge of monetary affairs enable it to operate its fine institutions successfully and prosperously.

The dedicated service of experts in various fields have made it possible for the church to put together a fine, modern, efficient, functional organization.

All this is well and good. No doubt much of it is even necessary. But tell me something. Where are the church's experts at loving?

Where are those who are skilled at meeting the deep, heart needs of frightened, anxious men and women living in a dying world. Where are those who care? Those who understand? Those who have time to listen? Those who know how to sympathize, empathize?

Confronted one day on a street corner by a preacher

17

who insisted that "God loved him," a young Harlem youth complained, "I'm sick and tired of hearing people talk about love. I want to see love with skin on it."

Is there anyone in the church who wants to help him?

Where are the experts at putting the love of God into words like Jesus could? Words that fit the vocabulary of a rough fisherman or an uneducated prostitute.

Where are those who are able to communicate the love of God instantly by the very expression of the face? By the tone of the voice?

Where, oh, where are the experts at loving? Perishing humanity awaits their long overdue entrance on the stage of man's deepest need.

The world needs nothing else so much as human beings showing the Saviour's love to each other. All heaven waits for men and women through whom God can reveal this enormous power of Christianity.

God is love. Are you?

3

EXPERTS AT LOVING

"Therefore with lovingkindness have I drawn
thee." Jeremiah 31:3.

One morning a hospital chaplain and friend of mine
walked into the room of a recently admitted woman.
Fiftyish, plump, and graying, the lady he found
appeared not only to be ill but to be very anxious and
distraught.

Stepping to her bedside, he began in his kindly way
to introduce himself.

Before he could even finish accomplishing this, the
woman burst out, "I don't want to see any preachers. I
have my own church. I like the way I believe, and I
don't want to be told anything else. I don't want you to
visit me while I am here in this hospital. Please, just leave
me alone."

The chaplain quietly started to turn. Then he paused
and gently said, "I didn't come here to preach at you. I
just came by to love you."

The startled patient was taken aback for a moment.
Then she relaxed, smiled, and said, "Well, come in and
sit down then. I can use a lot of that right now!"

During the patient's prolonged stay in the hospital

my friend returned daily to visit this woman because she wanted him to. A real friendship, a real relationship developed between them. He later said he felt as though this particular patient had been someone to whom he had been able to provide a significant spiritual ministry before the time for her discharge came.

Psychology has made it dramatically clear that the greatest and most urgent need of every human being is to be loved and accepted. Everything else in a person's life hinges on whether or not this need is being met—and how well it is being met.

God Himself has implanted this deep desire for sympathy and fellowship in the hearts of all. It is actually His universal gift to His children. It is a reality even in the strongest, even in the most self-sufficient.

Christ, in His hour of agony and trial in Gethsemane, longed for the sympathy of His disciples. He yearned for someone just to be there, to care, and to understand. Tragically, there was not even one.

The aggressive, independent apostle Paul often yearned for sympathy and companionship as he pressed on in his difficult, lonely, pioneering work for God.

God built the consuming desire to be loved into us all for a purpose. It is on the beachhead of this need that the Father makes His landing in our lives.

Everyone who encounters God does so in the process of seeking to have his own pressing need for love and acceptance fulfilled. On this level the Father draws all men to Himself.

On this level also Christians must base their efforts to establish the kingdom of God in the hearts of their fellowmen. Every person who will be saved will be saved through love. And this begins with God. "I have loved thee with an everlasting love; therefore with lovingkindness have I drawn thee." Jeremiah 31:3.

Love alone breaks down barriers. Love alone opens the doors of men's hearts to truth as it ministers to their greatest need. It is the one thing that everyone, like the woman in the hospital, "can sure use a lot of."

The popular song says it well: "What the world needs now is love, sweet love; it's the only thing there's just too little of."

God had enough love to meet the needs of a love-starved world. He has enough now to go around—in abundance.

There is just one problem.

Love is not real—it is of no value—unless it is expressed. For reasons known only to Him, *God has made Himself dependent on His people to express His love.* He puts His priceless treasure in earthen vessels. He has chosen human beings to communicate His blessings to the world. He intends His glory to shine through them to dispel the darkness of sin. God wants human beings to meet the sinful and the needy in *loving* ministry and lead them to Him.

God uses man as the medium to communicate the warmth of His love to the world. "The spirit of man is the candle of the Lord." Proverbs 20:27.

How terrible that, more often than not, God's people have failed in their unique divinely assigned role. They have miserably failed at expressing His love as it might be expressed. Selfishness and coldness have almost extinguished the fire of love. Many who claim to be

Christians have forgotten that God expects them to represent Christ.

What does representing Christ mean? It means nothing more and nothing less than expressing the love of God to people as Jesus did. This was what drew all men to Him. The loving expression on His face, the beauty of His character as revealed through His look and tone, drew to Him anyone who was not hardened in unbelief.

The abundant love of God was Christ's favorite theme. He talked it, He lived it, He *was* it. This marvelous, joyful insight into what God was really like was Christ's own special gift to men. This living truth, revealing how the Father longs to meet the keenest need of men, was what He had come to share.

This same precious knowledge about God, this love-experience with God, is the great gift committed to His people. And this He earnestly desires His followers to communicate to the world.

Every Christian is to be a love communicator!

Somewhere, somehow, this divine vision the Father has for us has nearly been lost. We tend to emphasize that which is less vital.

The greatest sin is the easiest to commit. It is the most subtle of all. It is the hardest to recognize in oneself. Society is quick to bring a murderer to face his crime. An adulterer knows in his heart that he is a cheat. The rational thief usually knows his actions are not moral or right. But to the one who breaks the law of love it is often only the stillest and smallest voice of conscience that may be heard by the calloused heart. And this gentle voice can be easily silenced. Permanently.

Because of the human proclivity that constantly urges one to live only for himself, callousness and insensitivity grow in us like a hidden cancer. We become indifferent to the needs of others, hardly aware that this is happening.

For example a doctor may become so accustomed to the routine of his work and grow so calloused and clinical that before long he is not treating patients but is merely dispensing professional first aid to stiff backs, peptic ulcers, and broken tibiae. He does not sense a healing ministry to *people.* And all the while nine tenths of the people who come to him with fears, anxieties, and frustrations have greater needs than can be cured with pill or knife.

Preachers are not immune to the greatest sin either. A pastor may wear out a Volkswagen a year operating a "good church program." He can balance budgets, set up committees, and preach Biblically correct sermons on the state of the dead while totally ignoring the state of the living: the people in his flock with real needs; people who want *someone,* at least the pastor, to be a person who really cares—a person who tries to understand. They want someone who is willing to talk with them about the things in life that really matter—someone who will pray with them and for them more than in the dutiful, part-of-the-yearly-twenty-minute-visit sort of routine way.

It is easy for a pastor to have the inner feeling that he cannot be a success as a minister unless he can "work up" to that "big church" someday. Better yet, goes the traditional philosophy, is getting behind a desk in a denominational administrative position. Here, according to conventional thinking, one can have the privilege of truly serving the Lord in a mighty, effective way.

Though such positions may be necessary to the carrying out of the practical work of the church, and though it is necessary for some to serve in this way, it is nonetheless true that such an office can very easily and conveniently be made a place remote from people and their real heart-needs.

Speaking of this tendency toward indifference to others, Dr. David Duffie says this in his book *Psychology and the Christian Religion:* "Sometimes the doctor shows more interest in making a scientific diagnosis than in helping a fellow human being. He herein becomes a 'good' scientist, but a poor doctor. A similar temptation confronts the clergyman. He may be so zealous of pure doctrine that he neglects its loving application to the individual soul, thereby tending to become a 'good' theologian, but a poor minister." Page 13.

No one *in any position or relationship* is immune to the tendency to be uncaring about others. Yet our failure to love, our inhumanity toward each other, is our greatest sin.

The word "inhumanity" usually provokes thoughts of some helplessly bound victim being tortured. It creates visions of thumbscrews and faggot-circled stakes. It brings to mind barbaric practices like those of the ancient Mongols.

They had the nasty habit of tying a horse to each arm and each leg of someone they wanted to dispose of. The four powerful animals, whipped off at a gallop in different directions, would then tear the hapless person into four pieces.

I have always thought of this sort of thing as being real cruelty, a prime example of "man's inhumanity to man." I failed to understand how the accusation could ever be leveled at *me* that *my* greatest sin was my inhumanity to my fellowman.

After all, I did not think of myself as the sort of person who would delight in torturing someone. I did not consider myself especially cruel by nature. That statement did not prick my conscience, because I was certain I could never be guilty of such a charge.

Only when I came to understand thoroughly that Christianity is actually nothing more and nothing less than what Christ clearly *said* it was, loving God and loving people by ministering to their needs, could I understand how my greatest sin might truly be what I have been told it is.

If Christianity is showing the tenderest affection for each other, then the very opposite of Christianity is failing to love.

From this perspective I caught a glimpse of my lack of love. I saw how frequently I had failed at caring about anyone but myself. I came to see that I was walking almost totally "in my own way." I discovered that according to the Bible definition, I was living deep in selfish sinfulness. All the while, of course, I was carefully keeping all God's commandments and living a "good," "moral" life.

The realization came that it was *not what I was doing* that was so bad. It was what I was failing to do, what I was failing to be to others, that was so tragically wrong.

Finally, seeing my real self, I could only cry, "Father, forgive my inhumanity toward my fellowmen."

4

WHAT IS LOVE?

"Jesus said unto him, Thou shalt love—"
Matthew 22:37.

More preconceptions and misconceptions seem to exist about love than anything else. One of the finest things God can do for you and me is to show us that love is not what we may have always imagined it to be.

To many, love is best described as a warm feeling for someone else. It is commonly believed that if you do not feel good or affectionate or compassionate toward another you do not love that individual.

This is a definition of *human* love. It is a false definition of *Christian* love. Christian love is not merely an emotion. It is instead *a consciously chosen attitude of a mind given over to God. A determined set of a will submitted to God.*

Loving is simply using one's God-given power of choice to say or do that which is in the best interest and for the best good of another person. Regardless of feeling.

Pure and holy affection is not a feeling. It is a principle.

God's supreme command is not "thou shalt feel

loving" but "thou shalt love." As long as our mind continues to function, we can obey that command. We do it by *choosing* to love Him and to love others.

Many struggling Christians bear serious concern about how they *feel* toward God. A great number are disappointed and discouraged because they never seem to experience the depth of feeling they think a good Christian should have toward Him. They constantly feel guilty because the amount of affection, the degree of warmth, they have toward God often is so slight.

Those in this dilemma know that they are supposed to love God more than anything or anyone else. Yet somehow they cannot manage to develop for Him even the amount of feeling they have for some people, no matter how they try. Not a few have become so discouraged over this seeming inability that they have given up Christianity. They concluded that they would never be able to care as much about God as they felt they were supposed to. Thus they assumed there was no hope for them.

Facing this quandary myself, I finally had to admit that I have a deeper emotional attachment for my wife than I do for God. I often feel warmer and more affectionate toward her than I do toward Him. My feelings for her definitely have a greater emotional strength than do my feelings for God.

However, I have come to see that in spite of this fact, I have used and continue to use the power of my mind for choosing to put God first in my life daily. I have decided and continue to decide to put Him ahead of myself, my wife, and my children. I now know that this means one important thing—I love Him the most!

27

If there were ever a conflict between doing my wife's will for me and what is God's, I would want to choose to put God's wishes above Kathy's. You see, then, though my emotional affection for her might be greater, my love for God is deeper. *Through the use of my will and by my actions* I demonstrate the priority I have chosen to give Him in my life.

Though God, whom we have not seen, may at times seem remote and distant, we may still love Him more than anyone or anything else by simply choosing to do so and then acting on that mental choice by putting His will first. Regardless of feelings.

The same divine principle applies to loving people. Even those to whom we may feel no affection. We may choose to love them by making the decision to do so with our minds and then by expressing the love we know God would want us to express through our words and actions. Regardless of feeling.

This is the only possible way to love the unlovely—those individuals who do absolutely nothing for us emotionally or who even cause us to have negative feelings toward them.

This is how Jesus Christ was able to persist in loving those who spit on Him—those who drew His blood with the raw edge of a scourge—those devil-possessed humans who murdered Him.

His actions and words clearly said to these despicable wretches, "You can do anything you wish to Me, but remember, *nothing, absolutely nothing* you can do to Me will be significant enough to make Me stop loving you. I am going to keep right on choosing to love you and talking to you and acting toward you as I do."

When the final crisis came, Jesus did not have some burning passion, some soulful, longing desire to be separated from His relationship with the Father and to die for totally unappealing, totally undeserving sinners. As a matter of fact, He prayed to God for a way *not* to go through with the ultimate sacrifice.

When the final agonizing decision was eventually made, it was *not* because Jesus wanted to go through with it. Rather it was because He loved the Father so much that He chose to do what God desired Him to. Come what may. Regardless of feelings.

The greatest act of love the universe has ever seen was not based on feelings! This incomprehensible miracle, which will be the awesome, unending contemplation of men and angels throughout the ceaseless ages of eternity, resulted simply from Someone's being willing to make the mental choice to put God's way first in spite of His own feeling and inclination.

By this unparalleled act Jesus Christ demonstrated to all men for all time what love really is.

This divine example compels us to go right on choosing to love those who we may have no feeling for, those who may oppose us, no matter what they may do or say to us or no matter how hateful they may become.

Such love is not humanly comprehensible. It is a distinct part of the mystery of Godliness. Try as they might, human hearts can never produce it. Yet in spite of this, Jesus boldly dared to bid His disciples, "Love your enemies." His command carries with it the assurance that we can successfully keep on loving when we feel like hating. He will give us the power to *act* toward all men in love. Just as He did.

Booker T. Washington, the noted black American educator, once said, "I will allow no man to drag me so low as to make me hate him."

Men who have followed in the steps of the Master and continued to love successfully in spite of great hostility and hatred toward them have always been able to do so because, like Mr. Washington, they have resolutely chosen to do nothing else. God has honored this choice and given them His supernatural power to carry this resolve out in word and action.

Christian loving, then, is a matter of mind over feelings. With the mind of Jesus in him, a man becomes free to choose the sort of unconditional, persistent love that can be limited by no kind of emotion.

A Christian then becomes free to act always in love toward people rather than reacting in response to their unloveliness.

What a priceless gift! This is what love is. Love in its fullest dimension. A liberated love, unshackled by fickle feeling!

A treasure bestowed on the sons of God. Now.

Your heritage and mine to share in a dying world.

LOVE WITHOUT AN "IF"

"But God commendeth his *love* toward us,
in that, *while we were yet sinners,* Christ
died for us." Romans 5:8.

It was going to be an interesting convention. Chaplains in training, accompanied by their supervisors, were coming in from institutions all over southern California. Some were working in mental hospitals, others in men's or women's prisons; and several, like me, were taking the course in a general hospital.

Since all of those involved in the program were either clergymen or theology students, I expected to see quite a conservative group of fellows. By the time of the first meeting I could tell that my assumption was correct. All were neatly dressed. Many wore black or dark-gray suits. Ties were narrow. Shoes were shined. The group looked exactly like I expected professional men, ministers, and graduate students to look.

With one exception—Paul.

When he walked into the room, I blinked. He reminded me of someone fresh out of a rock festival. His hair hung to his shoulders. Instead of a suit, he wore a pair of badly creased green corduroy trousers and an old red-and-white-striped T-shirt.

At first I thought he must be an inmate of one of the institutions and the chaplain had brought him along to demonstrate a counseling interview or something. Imagine my amazement when his turn came to introduce himself, and he stood to his feet and told us he was a theology student, taking chaplain's training. This fellow soon to be a minister or chaplain! Oh, no!

Inside me something began happening. Resentment began to build. What did this guy think he was proving? Coming to an important convention like that! It was an insult. Besides, how could he possibly visit with patients in the hospital he was assigned to when he wore his hair that way? I fumed to myself.

I found myself keenly disliking this strange character. *I wished that he would either leave or somehow change his appearance to be like the rest of us.*

At that point I am sure I could never have been a friend to Paul (for that was his name). My hostility toward him was just too strong. I am afraid it prevented me from really loving him as a fellow human being. It definitely canceled any chance of my being able to witness to him about any fuller dimension God might have in mind for his life.

You see, he was just too different from me. He did not meet my expectations. I did not approve of his appearance. *Therefore I did not approve of him.* I was not willing to accept him as he was.

My attitude might never have changed had I not found myself walking through the lobby beside Paul as a group of us returned from lunch. We introduced ourselves and began talking.

At least I was able to be honest with him.

I admitted to him that his appearance did not seem very appropriate to me and wondered aloud whether it interfered with his relationship to his patients.

In just a few minutes I learned much about Paul. He was open, friendly, and he spoke freely about himself. He explained that he had very little money and found it essential to work in order to get through school. His current employment involved playing evenings with a musical group in the Los Angeles area. A fact that he felt necessitated his hair style. His one good suit of clothes was reserved for when he was appearing on stage.

As he talked about his work in the hospital to which he was assigned, I could sense that he had a genuine concern for people and a real desire to help them.

In the sharing of experiences I felt myself growing close to Paul. By the time our conversation was over, my feelings of anger and resentment had faded away. We parted good friends. I still did not like his hair. Nor his unkempt appearance. *But I liked Paul and had begun to understand and accept him.*

The idea has kept haunting me. Suppose we had not talked? What if Paul had not had the patience to explain some of the things behind his way of life? Would I have gone on disliking him? How many times had I done this to someone else? Do I frequently write people off because they do not look the way I think they should? Or because they have beliefs that are different from mine? Or ideas I don't like? Or habits I don't approve? Are my relationships with people, the vehicle through which God wants to express His love to others, often limited because of my negative feelings and reactions

33

and lack of sympathy and understanding?

My experience with Paul that day has helped me perhaps more than anything else to understand with clear-cut certainty that real love is unconditional. Unconditional love is big enough and deep enough to accept people just as they are, simply because they exist. Sadly, this is a rare commodity, even in the church. Our human love is so conditional. Typically, we want people to meet certain qualifications before we become willing to love them.

Unfortunately the average person is programmed from birth to love only conditionally. Consequently we grow up feeling that we have to *earn* any love we get. Earn it by our good behavior, by agreeing to let someone else have their way, by giving someone what they want, or simply by just being "nice." This, of course, only breeds a circular kind of unprogressive conformity.

Since the impression is built deeply within us that we must "please" our parents, or our playmates, or anyone else for that matter, in order to be loved, we come to expect others to be willing to "please" us if *they* want *our* love.

This deep-seated attitude makes it humanly impossible for us to love anyone who disagrees with us, or believes differently, or acts differently from the way we think they should.

Because all men not only need to be loved, but also need to love, this often leads us in frantic efforts to manipulate people. To try to change them. To make them over into what *we* want them to be so that then we can love them. Thus we see people everywhere trying to change, manipulate, dominate, and control each other.

Unfortunately, too, this is frequently the subconscious motive in much so-called "witnessing." We feel assigned to go out and *change* the world—to change people so that we can love them and God can love them and, if they actually change enough, "save" them.

If you and I are doing something like this, we are guilty of gross misrepresentation of divine character. We are busy representing to people that God's love, like ours, is conditional.

The good news is that it is not!

We may think it is. We may have had this seriously mistaken concept ever since the time we heard Mother say, after we had been especially obnoxious, "You naughty boy. Don't you know that Jesus can't love you when you behave this way?" These people neither grasp nor experience the unconditional depth of God's love.

Yet through the years the influence of such people molds our plastic impressions. And eventually we come to convey clearly the false and dangerous assumption that people must perform in certain ways to be eligible to receive the love of God!

This is not the message the Father has given us to bear! God has not assigned any of us to the task of changing people. He only requests and commands that we love them. Just as they are. As He does.

During His earthly ministry, Jesus Christ never attempted to manipulate anyone. His message was not, "Change so that the Father can love you!" or "Change so that the Father can save you!" Men His marvelous life touched *did not repent so that He would love them.* They repented and forsook sin and began to change *because He did love them.* Lavishly! Unconditionally!

Christ's love for people was so thorough, so genuine, so spontaneous that He could constantly accept them just as they were. Sins and all.

Jesus had every reason to confine His ministry to the "nice" people in society. To those who had the blessing and approval of their peers. Those who dressed well and bathed often and whose reputation was as clean as their appearance.

He could have easily found excellent excuses for not associating with a person like Mary Magdalene. After all, He could have reasoned, why should He jeopardize His position, His influence, by being seen fraternizing with a streetwalker? It might reflect on the purity of His character. It could hinder His ministry to someone more deserving. Why should He waste His time on the chaff of society when He had only a few short months to accomplish His important task on earth?

Could He not easily have concluded that it would be more appropriate to send a lady Bible worker to counsel with her? He could have tipped off the temple authorities. They had ways of taking care of such scandalous people. Perhaps the public health department could have been informed.

Fortunately, for her and for us, the Saviour put no limit on His love. It was just as available to a drunkard or a thief or a prostitute as to anyone else. It was the love of God that knows no barriers. A love that does not condemn, but accepts. A love that does not reject and rebuke, but lifts and heals.

When that short life of His had been lived so well in such dynamic compassion, it was laid down in the most marvelous demonstration of unconditional love that the universe has ever seen or will ever see.

"But God commendeth his *love* toward us, in that, *while we were yet sinners,* Christ died for us." Romans 5:8.

In the light of God's willingness to love us so much and forgive us so much, just as we are, in our pitiful state of sinfulness and wretchedness, it is totally unacceptable that we should expect anyone else to make any changes or meet any qualifications before we are willing to consider them worthy of our puny human love.

To do this is far more deplorable even than the shameful action of the debtor in Jesus' story:

Through mismanagement this fellow had accumulated debts totaling over six million dollars as he handled some of the important finances of his country's government. The merciful king canceled all these obligations which had been charged to him personally. He wiped the slate clean, thus preventing the debtor and his wife and children from being sold into slavery on the auction block.

The very same day this man, to whom so much mercy and forgiveness had been extended, encountered an individual who owed him the sum of one day's wages.

Grabbing the man who owed him the small sum, the recently pardoned debtor demanded immediate repayment. In spite of the man's pleas that he would repay as soon as he could, the creditor had him imprisoned. This of course made it impossible for the money to be repaid. But it gave the recently pardoned debtor the satisfaction of revenge.

The king soon learned. He rebuked the unforgiving servant, put him back under his formidable obligation, and sentenced him to punishment. The words of the king's rebuke are of priceless value to all of us unforgiving, unaccepting, undeserving sinners:

"Shouldest not thou also have had *compassion* on thy fellowservant, even as I had pity on thee?" Matthew 18:33.

If God is willing to love and accept me just as I am—selfish, hostile, hateful, rebellious, unkind, critical, disobedient, disbelieving—who am I to be critical, unaccepting, and unloving of a fellow struggler?

In Shakespeare's words, "Forbear to judge, for we are sinners all."

The incomprehensible fact that God's unconditional love would cause Him to completely forgive a totally undeserving Douglas Cooper takes my breath away. How can I now speak a single, harsh, judgmental word toward another person? No matter how much I happen to disapprove of how he appears. Or what he does. Or what he believes.

My debt to God is so enormous, and the grievances I come up with against others are so ridiculously puny and small in comparison, that from this humbling perspective I am absolutely compelled to allow them to evaporate in the overwhelming warmth of the Father's deep compassion.

Only when I take this step am I ready to begin learning how to reflect His style of love to other people.

The love of God is the only free love that exists anywhere. Without God, human love, no matter how professedly pure, no matter how deep the degree of emotion that accompanies it, always has a qualification, an "if," a price tag attached.

This destroys its potential to meet anything but the surface needs of others. It cannot heal. It cannot uplift. It cannot save. It is limited to loving only the "lovable" and only as long as they remain "lovable." Its inadequacy eventually leaves men to perish without hope.

In Katherine Anne Porter's *Ship of Fools* one of the characters, not an especially lovable type, bitterly and compulsively cries out, "Love me. Love me in spite of all! Whether or not I love you, whether I am fit to love, whether you are able to love, even if there is no such thing as love, love me!"

This secret plea lies deep within the hearts of every person who does not know his Father's love. No human being can answer it by himself. But when you and I can respond affirmatively to this desperate, though often unexpressed, call we may be assured that God is working in us and through us to share His saving, unconditional love with the world.

"Love ye therefore the stranger: for ye were strangers in the land of Egypt." Deuteronomy 10:19.

6
LOVING THE DIFFICULT TO LOVE

"But I say unto you . . . Love your enemies.
. . . For if ye love them which love you,
what thank have ye?" Luke 6:27, 32.

Two psychiatrists, who maintained offices in the same building, often rode up together on the same elevator in the morning. The one who got off first, invariably turned around and spat on his colleague. The other would pull out his handkerchief and wipe his face and suit before getting off on a higher floor.

After watching this daily occurrence for some time, the elevator operator's curiosity finally got to him. One day, after he had let the first psychiatrist off at his proper floor, he said to the other, "Doctor, I just don't understand it. Tell me, why does your colleague spit on you every morning?"

"Oh, I don't know," replied the psychiatrist. "That's *his* problem!"

It is rather popular to be "accepting" in today's society. At least surface tolerance for other's viewpoints, beliefs, and behavior is becoming increasingly common. The tale of the two psychiatrists simply illustrates, however, the insufficiency of acceptance just for the sake of acceptance. A tolerant attitude toward people is necessary. But inadequate.

Imagine our plight if God had merely accepted us for what we are, sinners, and had done nothing to remedy our situation.

Likewise, our tolerant psychiatrist should have not only taken in stride his fellow practitioner's unusual behavior pattern. He should have also cared enough about the man to endeavor to help him.

He was quite good at *accepting* the unlovely. But he was a failure at *ministering* or helping.

Christians have the same difficulty.

Tolerating someone who may irritate us, or who may be unappealing to us is one thing. After all, *they* have *problems*, we reason. We must try to tolerate their deficiencies.

But as for becoming actually involved *with* them *in* their problems in a loving, caring way and assisting them toward wholeness, mentally, physically, or spiritually— well, this is something else. This demands something more. A great deal more. It is seldom done.

We tend rather to restrict our interest to only the "fun" people, the attractive people. Those who smell nice, who exhibit pleasant behavior, speech, and modes —those who dress well, who keep their hair carefully combed and their teeth brushed.

We covet their company. We like to ask them to an after-church dinner. These are "our" type of people. We have much in common with them. They think like we do. They appeal to us.

That leaves the old, the ugly, the boring, the embarrassing, the intellectually inferior. That leaves those we judge immoral or otherwise undesirable. These we leave alone at church services and social functions.

Oh, we manage the token gestures. The recognition of their existence. The halfhearted handshake. The guilty, nervous, condescendingly toned question about their health. The forced interest in what they tell us. But all the while we make it perfectly clear that we expect them to keep their distance and to know their place. The pet at home fares as well or better.

Some we even feel justified in rejecting. Like the hostile. Or the critical. Those who seem always to cause tension and frustration because of their eternal negativism. Those who seem forever spitting on people with words. Those who are repugnant because they talk too much. Those who make us uncomfortable because they talk too little. The crude. The flippant. The superegotistical.

To us, these unappealing, unlovely souls we justify ourselves in rejecting.

Can we not only tolerate and accept such people, but also love them and minister to them as well?

Others offer a different challenge to our ability to love. Those we expect always to be lovable and deserving of our love. Those we think we can always trust and depend on to be worthy of our affection. Like our wives, or our husbands, or our children, or our best friend, or our pastor. How do we react when they, too, suddenly become unlovable in our eyes? Will this then cause us to fail at loving—when they for some reason stop being their usual, pleasant selves?

He was one of the kindest, most considerate persons I have met. This pastor had the respect of everyone who knew him. Middle-aged, but still full of seemingly limitless energy and enthusiasm, he carried about him an air of mature authority and vigorous aggressiveness. This he channeled into positive avenues of ministry to his church and the people he served. He was understanding. I never knew him to fail to be genuinely pleasant and patient with everyone he dealt with. Except once.

I was a staff member at a week-long church camp for youngsters. The camp had turned out to be a trying experience. The weather was bad. The rain fell and the wind blew the entire time, causing frustration when many outdoor events and activities had to be cancelled.

Tents leaked. Colds developed. Campers complained. A general bad scene. The day we were to break camp the elements decided to stage an impressive grand finale. Heavy gusts of wind escorted by drenching rains hit at just the time the camp director, this pastor, was hurriedly attempting to organize everyone to accomplish the necessary tasks prior to our much anticipated departure.

Some of the youngsters were more intent on staying dry and as warm as possible than on tackling their camp duties that dreadful morning. Even some of the adult staff members showed a marked eagerness to tend in more detail to the work that would keep them inside or near a campfire.

The director's prodding motivated few in the camp. We had a schedule to meet. The pastor in charge could envision the dreadful complications that would result if the camp were not in order in time for the youngsters to meet their rides home. He rushed about the grounds, doing much of the work himself, vainly

43

trying to get help. Thoroughly soaked, cold, and looking miserable, he pushed on.

I was, virtuously enough I suppose, out working in the rain myself. The director chanced to walk by as I was right in the middle of things. Immediately he noticed that I was not doing the job the way he had evidently planned. Perhaps he had felt he could rely on me, and now it suddenly appeared that I was letting him down too. I'm not sure what prompted him, but right then, the pastor became very "human." The set of his usually pleasant face became almost cruel in expression. There was a touch of fury in his eyes.

His body tense with anger, he strode closer to where I was standing, and in a harsh, disgusted tone, gave me a cutting reprimand. Then quickly he turned and walked away.

I did not try to defend or protest. Probably because I simply was not given the opportunity to, more than anything. Or perhaps because I was so surprised. I had just witnessed a strange but not infrequent phenomenon. I had seen the ordinarily lovable become unlovely.

Never before had this man given me one single reason to dislike him or to feel anything but the warmest affection for him. He had always had a full quotient of my love and respect.

Now I had an excuse to justify not loving him.

Needless to say, by evening, when the confusion was over, the pastor was the patient, pleasant person he usually was. Though he never verbally apologized, by his attitude and actions he made it clear he was sorry.

As long as time shall last, there will be occasions when even the most lovable persons in our lives may become temporarily hard to love. They may slip away momentarily from a dependent relationship on Jesus. Their old nature succeeds in flaunting itself.

What matters for us, then, is how well we do at loving at times like these. Will their behavior lead us to respond in kind? Will we react negatively ourselves because an "excuse" arises? Can they do or say something capable of causing us to fail at loving?

It has been said that the hardest work in the world is loving people. This is true because always it means loving sinners, for all are. It means loving the wicked, the selfish, the deceitful, the proud, the cross, the ungrateful, the irritable, because this is the stuff of fallen human nature. All too frequently these characteristics have a way of revealing themselves. Even in those we expect or even would like to *demand* better of.

We must come to admit honestly that you and I are just totally incapable of loving such sinners. This is bad news if your wife or husband happens to be one. Or if your children turn out to be. Or your pastor. Or the guy in the next office. Or the old lady next door.

With our ability to love only conditionally, we are quite incapable of loving flagrantly imperfect souls. They are sure to disappoint us, to fail to meet the criteria we set up before we will dispense our human love.

Since all of our fellow mortals—including the ones we marry, or give birth to, or hear in church—are imperfect in nature, we cannot have unfailing, unvarying love for any of them. Not ourselves.

However, a Christian cannot read his Bible for long without recognizing that it exhorts us to be *more* than ourselves, more than human. It incessantly calls us to a higher and holier way of life. It plainly says that Jesus Christ wants to get inside us and do something supernatural.

Without apology the Scriptures state that we have actually not accomplished anything if we can only succeed at loving the lovely. "For if ye love them which love you, what thank have ye? for sinners also love those that love them." Luke 6:32.

The Word of God points us beyond the "natural affection" to the unlimited, undiminishing, unchangeable love the Father wants to put in us. A phenomenal, humanly incomprehensible sort of love. A love that will make it possible to love the temporarily or even permanently difficult to love.

Marvelously this unique quality is bestowed simply as a gift. It is the product of a personal, saving relationship with Jesus.

Unselfish love is the best gift God can give. This love does not result from impulse. It is a divine principle. It is a permanent power. Those who do not receive Jesus cannot originate or produce it. Only those who submit to the love of Jesus can show it to others.

When Paul tells of the all-important fruits of the Spirit of God at work in the lives of Christians (Galatians 5:22, 23), he places love at the apex. It is always produced spontaneously by the power of God in those captured by His love. His Spirit gives us the resources from within to live out the pattern of divine love.

So often, out of a sense of duty or guilt, we do try to love the difficult-to-love. But it is all so futile. We finally must come to the true but painful insight that our ever being able to love people well of ourselves is just as impossible as our being able to find salvation of ourselves. Even no amount of sincere effort will ever accomplish it. Something else is needed first.

We don't need to begin by trying to love one another. We need the love of Christ in our heart first. When self is submerged in Christ, true love springs forth spontaneously.

What a relief! What a load taken off the back! I have been liberated from the pressure of doing something I know I *must* do, yet am humanly incapable of doing! I now know that that which is so vitally essential, yet that which I can never hope to accomplish, is made available to me through the marvelous provision of my Saviour!

Believe me, a dramatically, but unfortunately all-too-often-overlooked part of the good news of the gospel of Jesus is that *it makes impossible love possible for you and me.*

If we look to Jesus, we can see brighter and clearer views of God. And by seeing God we become changed to be like Him. Goodness, love for other human beings, becomes a natural instinct.

Thus you and I may become supernatural lovers!

7

LOVE IS DOING

"Trust in the Lord, and *do* good." Psalm 37:3.

Jesus Christ revealed one of our finest insights into the nature of love in His attempt one day to help a certain lawyer. He was a man who, like many, could mouth the right words about the importance of love; but he had no concept of *how* to love.

Though the lawyer rejected Jesus' message at that time, the story has come down through the centuries as an unparalleled example of how God defines real love.

Here it is in the Cotton Patch Version:

"One day a teacher of an adult Bible class got up and tested him with this question: 'Doctor, what does one do to be saved?'

"Jesus replied, 'What does the Bible say? How do you interpret it?'

"The teacher answered, 'Love your God with all your heart and with all your soul and with all your physical strength and with all your mind; and love your neighbor as yourself.'

" 'That is correct,' answered Jesus. 'Make a habit of this and you'll be saved.'

"But the Sunday school teacher, trying to save face, asked, 'But...but...but...just who *is* my neighbor?'

"Then Jesus laid into him and said, 'A man was going from Atlanta to Albany and some gangsters held him up. When they had robbed him of his wallet and brand-new suit, they beat him up and drove off in his car, leaving him unconscious on the shoulder of the highway.

" 'Now it just so happened that a white preacher was going down that same highway. When he saw the fellow, he stepped on the gas and went scooting by.

" 'Shortly afterwards a white Gospel song leader came down the road, and when he saw what had happened, he too stepped on the gas.

" 'Then a black man traveling that way came upon the fellow, and what he saw moved him to tears. He stopped and bound up his wounds as best he could, drew some water from his water-jug to wipe away the blood and then laid him on the back seat. He drove on into Albany and took him to the hospital and said to the nurse, "You all take good care of this white man I found on the highway. Here's the only two dollars I got, but you all keep account of what he owes, and if he can't pay it, I'll settle up with you when I make a payday."

" 'Now if you had been the man held up by the gangsters, which of these three—the white preacher, the white song leader, or the black man—would you consider to have been your neighbor?'

"The teacher of the adult Bible class said, 'Why, of course, the nig—I mean, er...well, er...the one who treated me kindly.'

"Jesus said, 'Well, then, *you* get going and start living

49

like that!' "—*The Cotton Patch Version of Luke and Acts,* pages 46, 47.

The Bible shows God's love for people in *action* on their behalf. Its writers stand in awe at the great *acts* of love. "Behold, what manner of love the Father hath bestowed upon us, that we should be called the sons of God." 1 John 3:1.

"But God commendeth his love toward us, in that, while we were yet sinners, Christ died for us." Romans 5:8.

"Greater love hath no man than this," Jesus said, "that a man lay down his life for his friends." John 15:13.

Christ knew that He could reveal the love of God best by putting it in the form of dynamic action. Of Himself He said, "The Son of man came not to be ministered unto, but to minister, and to give his life a ransom for many." Matthew 20:28.

Another reported of Him that, "He went about *doing* good, and healing all that were oppressed of the devil." Acts 10:38.

This challenging life-style God has in mind for His followers today. He wants us to love actively! But how often this divine vision escapes us.

George Small has written,

"I read
In a book
Where a man called
Christ
Went about doing good.
It is very disconcerting
To me

That I am so easily
Satisfied
With just
Going about."

Jesus Christ did good for no other reason than that He was good. To this kind of love, to this kind of doing good, He calls us. All too often any good that you and I are prompted to do is based on some ulterior motive. We do good for someone because they have done something "nice" for us. We do good for someone because we "know we should" and would "feel guilty if we didn't." Or worse yet, we may do good for someone in order to put them in a position of owing us a favor so that we can then exert the pressure that will manipulate them into doing what we want them to do or into becoming what we want them to become.

If we are going to love as Jesus did, we will never be found doing good in order to get our own way or in order to be rewarded. This is certainly a radical philosophy in this day of materialism and commercialism.

Writing in the *Review and Herald* magazine, Dr. Sakae Kubo states: "He [Jesus] did not make friends to get people to come to church. He did not heal or do good to get them to join His movement. Many did, to be sure—because they were attracted to His prodigal, spontaneous love. But their response was not the determining factor in His doing good.

"The story of the good Samaritan illustrates how we ought to do good. He did not look around to see if there were photographers or newspaper reporters present, nor did he examine the man to see if he was a good prospect

51

for his church, nor did he calculate that if he would be kind to him, he might become a Samaritan. No, he just saw a fellow man in need of help, and helped him out of the goodness of his own heart. His was goodness for goodness' own sake, with no ulterior motive."—*Review and Herald,* July 20, 1967, p. 3.

Jesus was love in action.

Christian love is love in action.

Keith Miller gives this simple but penetrating definition: "Christian love is simply an act of the kind God wants performed for another person's health and wholeness to help fulfill His will for that person. And my *performing* that act in Christ's perspective and concern is the *love,* not my warm feeling *about* doing it."—*A Second Touch,* page 86.

Love does good for people because they are there. Because they have a need. With no thought about what they will do for us in return. Nor even how we feel toward them. This is to love as Jesus loved. This is the love of God. This is what Christianity is all about.

No wonder the Bible says, "Pure religion . . . is this, To visit the fatherless and widows in their affliction." James 1:27.

Millenniums ago the psalmist counseled, "Trust in the Lord, and *do* good." Psalm 37:3. Clearly trust, faith, belief, is futile of itself. Too often the emphasis has been on *believing* to the exclusion of *doing.*

Like the lawyer, many need to see that the ability to enunciate correct theological truth and to proclaim prophetic promises can never be a substitute for expressing love in action.

In a unique way Jesus got this message across to

Peter. See John 21:15-17. After the disciples had enjoyed a meal prepared for them by their Master (love in action meeting a practical need), Christ interrupted the tranquillity with a bluntly startling question.

Looking straight into the eyes of the former fisherman, Christ said, Peter, "lovest thou me?"

The disciple was shocked that His Lord would ask such a thing. Had he not made it clear where he stood and where his loyalty lay? Did Jesus not know of the strength of his belief in Him?

Peter was deeply surprised and hurt. He immediately became defensive. Quickly he replied, "Yea, Lord; thou *knowest* that I love thee."

The way he responded shows that the disciple felt Christ was asking him an unfair and even foolish question. After all, was it not he, Peter, that Jesus had praised lavishly for his prompt answer on the occasion when the Master was quizzing His followers about His true identity?

Peter had demonstrated his unwavering belief in Jesus by proclaiming that He was the Christ, the Son of the living God.

Now the Lord seemed to be casting doubt on the purity of Peter's faith. How could this be?

If you or I had been in the Lord's place at the time, we would have undoubtedly answered Peter's concerned, hurt response with a typical, reassuring, "I love you too." Then we would have gone our way and let the matter drop. After all, we would not want to hurt the man's feelings. We would have handled it much as we do when our little children come to us saying, "I love you, Daddy." Usually the best sort of reply we can muster to that is a sugar-coated over-the-top-of-the-newspaper, "Daddy loves you too."

But if Christ had answered that day with a trite acceptance of the man's expression of love, Peter would have been cheated of a profound spiritual learning experience. And so would we.

He would have gone on like so many others, never understanding what love really is.

There is no question that Jesus knew that Peter had a strong belief in Him. He knew too that, in his human way, His disciple loved Him. The Lord was not questioning His disciple's loyalty that day, as Peter might have at first worried.

Instead of a token response to Peter's reply, Jesus stated in a simple three-word sentence an insight which said more to Peter and the others around that fire on the beach—and says more to us—about what love actually is than anyone or anything else ever can.

Gently but firmly the Saviour commanded, "Feed my sheep."

"Peter," He was saying, "there is something extremely important I want to teach you today. If you believe, if you love, *do something* about that love. Because you see, Peter, love is not just a nice emotion. Love is not just something you feel toward someone you happen to like, *love is something you do.*

"In other words, if you really love Me, Peter, if you are a for-real disciple of Mine, then this will be expressed and confirmed only by your demonstrating that love in active ministry to the needs of people."

Many think love is an automatic consequence of correct belief and careful obedience. Like Peter, they feel that their love is something above question. Particularly their devotion and their love to God. They think that their love is obviously all it should be because their belief and loyalty are in the right place. Just like Peter's.

No concept could more readily contribute to setting a church up for the Laodicean condition of calloused self-satisfaction. *No concept is more likely to subtly keep people from the kingdom of heaven.*

This attempt of Jesus to share the vital perspective about true love was among some of His very last words to His disciples before ascending to heaven. This fact demonstrated the importance He placed on true love.

He wants all to grasp the great and basic Christian principle of the imperative necessity of love expressed in action.

The Lord could have said many things to His disciples during their last meal together on earth. He could have reminded them of many important truths. He could have reviewed for them several basic doctrines.

Instead He concerned Himself with making certain that they comprehended one of the most vital elements of loving as God does. And we too.

When He comes again and sees His people once more face to face, Jesus Christ will interest Himself in how well human beings have understood and faithfully followed through on the dynamic insight He shared that day on the lakeshore:

"When the Son of man shall come in his glory, and all the holy angels with him, then shall he sit upon the throne of his glory: and before him shall be gathered all nations: and he shall separate them one from another, as a shepherd divideth his sheep from the goats: and he shall set the sheep on his right hand, but the goats on the left." Matthew 25:31-33.

Notice the shocking distinction in the eternal destinies of those who make up these two final different groups:

"Then shall the King say unto them on his right hand, Come, ye blessed of my Father, inherit the kingdom prepared for you from the foundation of the world." "Then shall he say also unto them on the left hand, Depart from me, ye cursed, into everlasting fire, prepared for the devil and his angels." Matthew 25:34, 41.

The pressing question is, of course, What makes the difference? Of all things, what determines whether one receives the matchless gift of eternal life or the punishing horror of eternal death?

What is the basis of the final divine judgment?

In terms a small child can understand, God paints a quick portrait of the only kind of people who will gain entrance into His marvelous eternal kingdom.

Why will certain ones be able to hear the welcome joyful words, "Come . . . inherit the kingdom"? Will it be because they have believed the correct truths and have obeyed the letter of the law?

No. God's invaluably priceless reward is bestowed on the basis of the kind of person one has become through his relation to Jesus Christ:

"For I was an hungred, and ye gave me meat: I was thirsty, and ye gave me drink: I was a stranger, and ye took me in: naked, and ye clothed me: I was sick, and ye visited me: I was in prison, and ye came unto me. Then shall the righteous answer him, saying, Lord, when saw we thee an hungred, and fed thee? or thirsty, and gave thee drink? When saw we thee a stranger, and took thee in? or naked, and clothed thee? or when saw we thee sick, or in prison, and came unto thee? And the King shall answer and say unto them, Verily I say unto you, Inasmuch as ye have done it unto one of the least of these my brethren, ye have done it unto me." Matthew 25:35-40.

On the authority of the Word of God, your readiness for eternal life, and mine, is simply and plainly shown by how well we have loved.

When God reviews the cases of all human beings who have ever lived, He does not ask what they have professed. Instead, He asks what they have done. Have they lived Christ's life? Have they lived for themselves or others? Have they busied themselves with giving, with deeds of kindness? Have they acted in love, preferring others before themselves, denying their own desires in order to bless others?

If the record shows that they have, then they will hear the words, "Well done." "Come, ye blessed of my Father, inherit the kingdom prepared for you from the foundation of the world."

The Bible does *not* say, "I was an hungred, and you suggested I check out the food stamp program." It says, "You *fed* me."

It does not say, "I was thirsty, and you shook your head over the shortage of good, pure water." It says, "You *gave* me drink."

It does not say, "I was a stranger, and you referred me to the proper welfare agency or directed me to the nearest YMCA." It says, "You *took* me in."

It does not say, "I was naked, and you felt

57

embarrassed and ignored me." It says, "You *clothed* me."

It does not say, "I was sick, and you, by your paying an honest income tax, supported the Medicare program." It says, "You *visited* me."

It does not say, "I was in prison, and you not only voted legislation for a penal rehabilitation program, but also mailed me some back copies of a church paper." It says, "You *came* unto me."

The all-wise Judge of the universe will say of those who will inherit His kingdom, "You love me, and you expressed that love. You made it real by *doing* something for someone else. Not because you were trying to earn My favor or theirs, but simply because they were *there* and they had a need. You fed my sheep."

Many who, much to their eternal despair, will be found in the group that lose out in the judgment will not be "bad" people. Their theology may have been right. Their church attendance remarkably and commendably regular.

But they will lose all!

Why?

Because they never put their love into action. They did nothing for God or others. The love they professed to have, and were certain they had, they never expressed. Therefore it was never there at all.

Tragically, they cannot be redeemed—because they were the kind of persons who failed to do good, and to share God's love.

At that time these do-nothings will have nothing to say. They will see the sin involved in their neglect. They will see that they have robbed God of lifelong service.

58

They will see that they have influenced none for good. They will see that they have brought nobody to Jesus. They will see that their content to do nothing for the Master receives no reward but eternal loss. Regardless of their claim to be followers of Christ, they will die with the wicked.

Here is the tragic picture of a group who, like Peter, *assumed* that they loved. People who always thought that love was just a selfish feeling and who never bothered to understand that love involves doing something for someone in need.

In the most marvelous demonstration of real love that the universe has ever seen, God made it indisputably clear once and for all that the very essence of *love*—is *action*.

8

LOVING IS TRUSTING

"Honour all men." 1 Peter 2:17.

In his book *The Spirit of Christ in Human Relationships* (Zondervan, 1968) James Bishop tells of an incident related to him in 1937 in Madras, India.

"Canon Goldsmith was a very devoted and much loved missionary of the Anglican Church in the city. One day he entrusted to his Indian servant a sum of money with which to buy supplies. But instead of buying and bringing the supplies, the servant disappeared with the money. Canon Goldsmith was much distressed. For days he searched for the man. Finally, finding him he went to him in deep humility and said, 'I am so sorry I paid you such small wages for your work that you had to do a thing like this. Come back and keep working for me and I will give you better pay.' The servant was completely overcome by this expression of love and confidence. He went back, thoroughly repented, and became Canon Goldsmith's devoted, trusted servant, friend, and brother for life."

How quickly you and I would have written off that thieving servant. More than likely we would have reported him to the police. His capture and punishment would have gratified us. We might even have complained to some of our fellow missionaries about "those people" who can never be trusted.

The way Canon Goldsmith treated his erring servant was not human. It was superhuman! It is our nature to want to cut off or see punished those who do us wrong. The desire to give them a second chance, to show trust in them again, is usually foreign to us. In almost a humorous way God once revealed the sham of our unforgiving, untrusting human natures: "I will not execute the fierceness of mine anger, I will not return to destroy Ephraim: for I am God, and not man." Hosea 11:9.

We must admit that only the Spirit of God at work inside a person can produce attitudes and compassionate actions like Canon Goldsmith exemplified. Only God's love in you and me can go right on trusting those who have disappointed us and may disappoint us again.

Jesus Christ was the most trusting Person there ever was. Jesus Christ was taken advantage of more than anyone else. Yet this did not stop Him from trusting. His life clearly shows us that it is far better to trust people and be betrayed than it is to cheat ourselves of real depth in our human relations by not trusting at all.

Jesus trusted Simon, the irritating, impetuous, boasting fisherman. He even trusted Zacchaeus, the shrewd, conniving, deceitful little tax collector. And Mary too. Mary the prostitute.

This trust made a decisive difference for these people. It became the doorway to their salvation.

Christ risked His trust. He trusted in costly ways that made Him openly vulnerable. His trust extended to

Judas, even though *He knew* Judas would betray Him! He trusted Judas with His money. He trusted him with His reputation. He even trusted Judas with His life. On all counts Judas betrayed His trust. And though Jesus knew this beforehand, He still trusted Judas.

And we, who have proved untrustworthy many times, are nonetheless redeemed by trust! God's unmerited trust in us.

Trust is an essential ingredient of Christian love. In fact, love does not exist without it. "Love is an act of faith," Erich Fromm has written, "and whoever is of little faith is also of little love."

Love works through trust. Trust serves as nothing else to show our fellowmen that we believe in their value. Trust communicates the worth or potential worth we see in others. Without trust we can do nothing for others.

A big part of our Christian "good news" is our message that people are extremely valuable. The human person, whoever he may be, is priceless beyond measure. God values the person so highly that He would have sent His Son to die for only one—any one of all humans who have ever lived.

In contrast to this, how callous we can be! We trample over the delicate tendrils of a person's feelings as if they did not exist. We speak cold words to the easily chilled spirits of those who desperately need our sympathy and understanding. We offhandedly reject ideas or suggestions that may mean everything to another person who has trusted us enough to share them with us. We think little or not at all of the heinousness of destroying another's precious dreams. We deflate expertly, almost effortlessly. We maul and mutilate human beings made in the image of God and respected by God and derive fun and satisfaction from it.

How thoughtless we are of each other! If we would only lower our egos before God and show kindness, courtesy, and pity for our fellow human beings, we would see one hundred decisions for God where we now see only one.

We must, through Jesus, come to see every person whom our lives touch as being utterly special, unique, and worthwhile. We must understand that each person deserves our best.

God offers His best to everyone. Regardless. To Him each has special, inestimable value.

"Why does God love us all so very much?" a Bible-class teacher asked her primary tots one day. There followed the silence of hard thinking. Then one little girl spoke up. "Because He has only one of each of us."

To know that God would have sent His Son to die for any one sinful human person, is to know something about the worth God places on each one of us.

If we could only comprehend the immense value of the individual! If we could only see each one as he really is—doubly priceless because God made each in His own image and because He redeemed each through the gift of His Son Jesus Christ!

Who can determine the value of one soul? Think of the Garden of Gethsemane where Christ suffered long hours of anguish and superhuman torture in behalf of each one of us. Think of our Saviour on the cross. Think of His despairing cry, "My God, my God, why hast thou forsaken me?" Mark 15:34. Think of His bloody head, His stabbed side, His ruined feet. Christ risked all. To redeem us humans He risked heaven itself. Knowing that for one sinner Christ would have died, you may then begin to estimate the value of one soul.

In communicating this sense of worth, we must trust. Through trust we can express to people the value or potential value they have. We can reveal to them the value we see in them by the degree of trust we show in them.

To invest our trust in a person says more plainly to him than anything else, "You are important. You have worth. I value you for what you are and for what you can become."

The Bible commands, "Honour all men." 1 Peter 2:17. This can be fulfilled only by trusting all men. There is nothing that honors someone more than our unvarying trust.

"Confident hope" defines trust. We have to be realistic about people; but regardless of how many mistakes they have made, we may express a "confident hope" to them that we feel they are capable of something better. We can actively demonstrate the value we see in people by trusting them. Our trust can inspire and motivate a person to become what they have not yet become.

As the psychologist Bonaro Overstree has said, "We are not only our brother's keeper; in countless large and small ways we are our brother's *maker*." Trust is the tool that God gives us to use to make men grow into His image as they come to see their potential as created and redeemed sons of His.

By the value we place on others, by our attitude toward them, we are capable of making them better or worse. Think of what the thieving servant became as a direct result of Canon Goldsmith's trust! Ralph Waldo Emerson once wrote, "Trust men and they will be true to you. Treat them greatly and they will show themselves great."

Every individual has certain attributes, certain qualities of character and personality, and certain abilities which will blossom with encouragement and confidence shown them. Jesus always looked for the best in people. He never dwelt on weak points. He always tried to bring the best to the surface. Through this He showed us one of the most exciting ministries of love.

Love always trusts and always places the most favorable interpretation on others' motives and acts. "This love of which I speak," the apostle Paul said, "looks for a way of being constructive." 1 Corinthians 13:4, Phillips.

Lawrence of Arabia was renowned for his ability to relate well with the Arab people. Few other foreigners had ever been able to do so. Asked once how he managed to accomplish this, he replied, "I treated every Arab as an Englishman."

We must look for good in others. We must expect it from them. We must treat them as if they had worth. This is the key to opening *their* confidence and trust in *us.* It is also the key to opening to them the gospel. How rare to look only for the best in others! How typical to look only for the worst!

Remember the reaction of the elder brother in the parable of the prodigal son? When the father, overjoyed at the wanderer's return, called a special feast to celebrate, the older son would have nothing to do with

65

it. The Scripture says, "And he was angry, and would not go in." Luke 15:28. His attitude showed with striking clarity that had he been in the father's place, he would have rejected the prodigal's return. So unaccepting was he that he did not even call his brother "brother," but coldly referred to him to his father as "thy son."

This suspicious attitude is the kind that would try to convince his father that the younger brother was just attempting to take advantage of the family's wealth and security again, pointing out what a fool the father will be to let himself get conned into taking back a profligate who can never again be trusted.

But the father does trust the prodigal son. In spite of the dreadful mistakes the young man has made and the wrongs he has done. To the father nothing is more valuable than his own boy, the one who was lost but is now found.

He gives him the very best—the finest robe, an expensive ring. He invites the neighbors and musicians to a special feast. Far from being ashamed of his son, he wants to *honor* this boy who is worth everything to him.

"Honour all men," says the Word. Even the prodigals. If we could only see people through the Father's eyes of infinite love, then we could look upon them all as His children, our brothers and sisters!

We may claim to be children of God; but if our claims are true, then our own brother who was lost and dead we must consider to be alive and found. He is bound to us by the closest ties, for God recognizes him as His son. But if we deny our relationship to him, we show that we are but hirelings in the household, not children in the family of God.

9

LIBERATED TO LOVE

"If the Son therefore shall make you free, ye shall be free indeed." John 8:36.

The spirit of man is the candle of the Lord. But it must be released, freed from the prison of selfishness, from the shackles of fear and conformity, before God can use it to warm the lives of others.

Only someone who is not bound by the influence and opinions of others, who is free to be totally and honestly himself in all situations, can communicate through his life the love of God to the fullest extent. Only a Christian can be an expert at loving, because it is only a Christian who can love himself well.

You see, love for others, the supernatural love that God puts in us, is structured so that it can be launched only from the pad of a deep love for one's own self. If this sounds strange, remember that Jesus commanded each of His men to "love thy neighbor *as thyself.*" He was emphasizing, without any of the usual apologies, this essential but timorously accepted principle of in-depth loving.

Christ knew that the ability of His disciples to live God's love in the world would be subtly thwarted, not so much by the unloveliness of those they were commanded to love, but rather by a security problem—the lack of security in their own lives that would be a result of their not having the proper concept and the right kind of self-love.

Jesus knew that those who are insecure do not possess the additional force of will or the emotional strength needed to love others well. The vitality that God would have them use to reach out and make connection in a ministry to other lives is so easily short-circuited by the draining pull of one's own fears, frustrations, guilts, and anxieties.

Self-love and free inner security are essential to loving others. If a person is insecure about himself, dislikes himself, or even hates himself, he cannot love others.

The Master views self-love as so essential that He presupposes it as a necessary condition of obedience. The Christian has been *commanded* to love others on the same basis that he loves himself. Thus the imperative of possessing self-love is to the Christian unavoidable.

Unfortunately, in spite of distantly sensing its importance, many are completely frightened and extremely uncomfortable with the concept of self-love. They feel guilty at the thought of its implementation or cultivation in their own lives. They never experienced it as the vital, positive force Jesus intends it to be. This drastically cripples their ability to function as love-communicators.

Dr. Robert H. Felix, former director of the National Institute of Mental Health in Washington, D.C., gave one of the least complicated definitions of self-love when he said, "Self-love is having a feeling of dignity, a feeling of belonging, a feeling of worth-whileness, a feeling of adequacy—yet a healthy sense of humility."

Jesus evidently visualized it as such a simple thing, so unaffected and so natural for the Christian, that He did not even bother to define it at all. He just presupposed it for all of us who believe we are His!

He knew that it is one of the finest gifts Christianity bestows. He knew that it comes free of charge, a part of the package to anyone who genuinely chooses to reach out to Him as Lord and Saviour and Friend. This is why it is only a Christian who can be an expert at loving well, because it is only a Christian who can love himself well. A Christian is given this freeing ability from God just as he is given the ability to love others. Both are just as much a gift from the Holy Spirit.

A non-Christian may sense the importance of self-love. Any thinking person who is psychologically informed can see its immense clinical significance, because repeated demonstrations show that the lack of self-love is one of the greatest contributors to mental illness.

"If people had a healthy love of themselves instead of carrying hidden burdens of self-contempt," Dr. Alexander Reid Martin, formerly of the Payne Whitney Psychiatric Clinic in New York, has stated, "our psychiatric case load would be cut in half."

A great part of the "good news"—but a part that we Christians are unfortunately not proclaiming as we could—is that God has an inestimably valuable gift of *self-love* waiting for every guilt-ridden, self-depreciating, insecure sinner.

Why are we so hesitant to tell them where it is?

Didn't Jesus have something to say about a lighter yoke and an easier burden?

Doesn't He have something to provide for those troubled souls whose life is often marked by futility and despair? Despair over what they are and over what they are not. Despair over what they want to accomplish but cannot. Despair over the deep need to give love which God has built into their very core but which they frustratingly cannot share—because they have no launching pad of self-love from which to direct it to others. Whole new dimensions in loving await them, but they never reach these levels because they have never been introduced to the only true Source of genuine self-love.

When we Christians get around to mentioning self-love, if we ever do, it is often in a hushed, apologetic way. We usually skip right over it and go on to elaborate on the virtues of "something more healthy and important," something we feel less uncomfortable talking about, like the virtue of loving God or others, or the virtue of obedience to the law.

But to avoid the Biblical concept of self-love is to deprive people of something they need in order to love others. For some persons this concept may be the most vital thing our Christianity enables us to share, because this may be the one thing they most need.

A non-Christian, though able to sense the importance of self-love, cannot achieve it to the necessary degree the Christian can. He can do this no more than he can love the unlovely or earn his own salvation. It is utterly impossible.

Jesus predicted that the world would marvel at the intensity of love displayed by His followers. "They will know we are Christians by our love," says a gospel song. This is so because Christians have the sort of divinely given self-love at their roots that frees them and powers them to project their love and God's love out into other lives. If you do not accept this gift of self-love, you cannot adequately display Christianity; you end up saying—by your life—something like "they will know we are Christians by our ethics" or "they will know we are Christians by our doctrinal purity."

But they won't.

A Christian first realizes self-love when he begins to grasp the immensity of God's unconditional love for him. The fire of God's all-inclusive, unwavering, totally accepting love is the one thing that can spark genuine self-love in a person. And the warmth of that heavenly fire is felt most from the hilltop of Calvary.

When a person begins to see that God loves him *that* much, even while he is yet a sinner, when he hears the voice of Jesus Christ addressing him from the cross and gently calling him "beloved," he comes to see himself in a new light. He gains a new sense of his own worth. He sees the value that God places on *him*.

Nothing in human history has demonstrated more vividly the value of a human being than the death of Jesus Christ for each person. Individually coming to believe in and comprehend the magnitude and intensity of that sacrifice is the one and only experience which can instill in a person the necessary foundation of healthy self-love.

In simple terms, I know I can love myself because I know that Jesus Christ loves me and calls me beloved. In fact, when I see myself this way, I have no choice but to love myself! After all, who am I to despise in any way someone whom God loves so much that He gave His only Son to die for him?

I know too that the Father loves me because He is love. Not because I am especially good or especially deserving. He loves me just as I am, frailties and all, sins and all, hang-ups and all. This knowledge, then, frees me to love myself in this way too. I can still love myself though I know that I am imperfect. I need not despise myself for my sins. I need not dislike myself for my mistakes. God does not. Why should I? After all, He is perfect and would have a right—if anyone would—to look down on me because of my imperfections.

Yet He does not. He does not approve of them, but He is willing to approve of me and accept me just as I am.

I, on the other hand, being imperfect, like the debtor in the parable, have even less a right than God does to look down on anyone who is not perfect, *including myself*.

To sum up, God has willingly forgiven me such an immense debt that in view of what He has done for me, I have no right to be unforgiving of myself! Again, to do so would be to contradict Him.

People are often driven to insanity because they "cannot forgive themselves" for something. Guilt is destroying multitudes today—physically, mentally, and spiritually. The world is full of discouraged, defeated people who intensely dislike themselves or what they have done. Their life is hell in the present tense because they are unable to forgive themselves.

How desperately they need to hear the good news

that they do not need to! God has already taken care of that! *He* has already forgiven them. When God forgives someone, they are really forgiven. All they need to do is to love themselves. As He loves them. Totally, unconditionally, unwaveringly. Jesus bought this privilege for them on the cross. He still gives it as a free gift to those who dare to believe in Him and what He did.

"But as many as received him, to them gave he power to become the sons of God." John 1:12.

You can love a son of God, can't you? Then you can love yourself, because you are one!

To be put right with God, to be justified by faith, is the greatest source of inner security, the greatest wellspring for self-love and self-acceptance there is.

"If the Son therefore shall make you free, ye shall be free indeed." John 8:36.

Fellow Christian, because God has forgiven you everything, you are now free to love yourself.

This alone sets you free to love others.

You have been liberated to love! You can now enter into a love-ministry to people that is superhuman because you have the true foundation from which to love. You can introduce people to God and His love now, because you are free to be yourself in Jesus Christ.

The person who has been forgiven everything by God does not need to "impress" others. He is free to concentrate on *loving* them! He does not need to struggle to gain their approval. He does not need to worry about performing or conforming in order to gain social acceptance. He is no longer compelled to seek human support or reassurance. He has been liberated

73

from such cobwebs of dependency and insecurity to minister to others.

If, however, a person does not fully accept and appreciate the freeing gift of self-love that God offers him, he will more than likely remain incapable of aggressively obeying His Lord's command to go and share what he has received. He will not have a dynamic witness. He will be fearful of an encounter with others in any depth emotionally or spiritually. He will tend to hold back. He will be hesitant about establishing communications and relationships with other people, because he is still afraid of being rejected. Rejection is always excruciatingly painful to those whose self-love quotient is low.

In writing about why people are so often afraid even to speak to each other or why they find it so difficult to trust one another, Ardis Whitman has said, "The main reason is that we are afraid. Watch a pair of stiff people sitting side by side on a plane or a train, each fearing to speak."

She quotes Rabbi Joshua Liebman as saying, "We are afraid of being disparaged, rejected, unmasked." *Christian Herald,* December, 1968.

Any person secure in the love of Jesus will not need to let his fear of people—his fear of rejection—stifle the God-given impulses to witness, to share, and to love. He will not need to expend his energy covering his imperfections and pretending to be something that he is not in order to try to gain the approval of others. Instead, he is perfectly free to be himself honestly, without mask or cover-up or apologetic rationalization.

His surrendered self-hood can be an unencumbered

channel of God's love and grace!

Of such a sense of release and freedom the non-Christian cannot even dream. Being *totally* free of the trappings of fear and insecurity is *totally* impossible for them. They may try all sorts of intellectual gymnastics to convince themselves that they are free and independent; they may even come to believe they are. But they are not. Some sophisticates today, through their keen psychological insights, feel they have matured to the point where they have achieved freedom from dependencies and insecurities. They are quick to flaunt their self-sufficiency. The truth is that they have more often than not simply exchanged one set of fears and dependencies for another set not quite so obvious. At least not to themselves.

Only Jesus sets people free to be themselves—as He created people to be. Without Him they are not. And cannot be.

Have you any real sense of what it means to be able to look face to face with any man and say, "A perfect God in heaven loves me so much that He has accepted me as I am. This gives me the right to expect that you, who share in my human imperfection, will be willing to grant me the same privilege."

A person who is justified by faith is not inferior to anyone! He need make no pretensions. He need offer no defenses.

"If God is for us, who can be against us? He did not even keep back his own Son, but offered him for us all!" "Who will accuse God's chosen people? God himself declares them not guilty!" Romans 8:31, 33, Today's English Version.

So there is no reason for us Christians to be afraid of anyone or to feel "put down" by anyone. That is good news! Even better news is the fact that this then frees us to love anyone and everyone!

"There is no fear in love; but perfect love casteth out fear." 1 John 4:18.

A crushing burden of fear and insecurity exists in the world because there is so little love. The fact that there is so little love is not God's fault. He is love, and He wants to fill the whole earth with His loving presence. The fault lies with you and me for not claiming more of God's love for ourselves and sharing it with others.

We might as well admit it. Our fear of people has too often been the barrier that has kept us from loving them for Jesus.

How unnecessary! How unnecessary that we who claim to have found favor with God and to have been accepted by Him as His sons and daughters should be afraid of people. We need more of the bold secure faith of Jacob, who wrestled through the night with the Lord until he received the assurance of sins forgiven and blessings granted. Jacob prevailed with God. This assured him that he would prevail with men. He no longer feared his brother's anger. The Lord became His defense.

God wants to assure you that you can prevail with men also. Not to use or abuse them, but to love them well—for Him. To reject this assurance, this promise, this gift, is to succumb to a sense of fear and inadequacy. This keeps you from freely loving others.

"There's nothing I'm afraid of like scared people," wrote Robert Frost.

Anyone who feels inferior and inadequate cannot

relate well to others. To us Christians who see our primary purpose in this world as relating in depth to others and sharing the love and truth of God through such relationships, this is a serious matter.

How fortunate we are that the Father provides security for the insecure. Fearlessness for the fearful. He gives His own the strength from within that keeps them from being crushed by what others think or say about them or do to them. "In God have I put my trust: I will not be afraid what man can do unto me." Psalm 56:11.

"Thou shalt be hid from the scourge of the tongue; neither shalt thou be afraid of destruction when it cometh. At destruction and famine thou shalt laugh." Job 5:21, 22. Now someone who can do *that* is secure! God says you can!

Why? Because you are justified by faith. No one, no thing, can touch you. You have prevailed with the God of heaven. You need not now fear men or circumstances of any sort. *You are liberated to love.*

There is no freer person anywhere than the one who has learned how to love. The impact of even one such life is infinite. No limit to its constructive power for good exists.

A man once described a woman he had known this way: "She came to meet everyone with both hands out. You felt as if she were saying, 'How I trust you! I feel so fine just being with you!' You went away feeling as if you could do anything you tried after you had been with her."

The well-known Christian author, Eugenia Price, in one of her books writes of the impact that a friend has had on her life—a friend who is obviously secure in

77

self-love and self-confidence and in God's love:

"I have been singularly fortunate to have had an older friend for all the years of my Christian life who also has helped free me by her love. . . . Her *love* has been the continuing help I needed to go on daring to learn to fly in the love of God on my own. She is unshockable, totally uncondemning, full of the holy humor of God Himself, and she loves me. Of this I have no doubt whatever. Because I know she would never condemn me for anything, I am thrown directly onto God for my need of conviction. Her love stimulates my mind, stretches me inside where I need to be stretched, and keeps me actively searching the wider place of freedom in God for more and more knowledge of Him."—*Make Love Your Aim* (Zondervan, 1967), page 40.

Eugenia Price is fortunate enough to have a friend who is helping her to know God more personally.

How desperately the Father longs for those who will do the same for Him. He knows that many of His lost children simply cannot experience His love apart from people.

He is waiting for us to begin loving them, *as we love ourselves.*

10

DARE TO LOVE NOW

"Woe unto you, when all men shall speak
well of you." Luke 6:26.

If your life is serene and comfortable, if all your
relationships with other people are generally smooth,
and if you do not feel that you have any enemies, maybe
you are not yet fully a Christian!

Some individuals take pride in the fact that they get
along amiably with everyone. They often consider this a
strong indication of their successful spiritual experience.
To them, working at winning the approval and keeping
the favor of as many people as they possibly can is
all-important. They assume that a Christian is someone
who should be liked by everyone.

The Bible, however, places something ahead of
"winning friends and influencing people." That is, doing
the will of God. That is to come first.

Jesus said that it was His "meat . . . to do the will of
him that sent me." That was paramount in all He did
and said. He lived for that. The Master recognized that
this policy would often conflict with what men might
want Him to do or to be. He warned His followers early
that anyone who would choose to elevate God's will

above everything and everyone else in life—as He was doing—could expect to find themselves at cross purposes with the world. Without flinching or apologizing, He told them, "I came not to send peace, but a sword. For I am come to set a man at variance against his father, and the daughter against her mother. . . . And a man's foes shall be they of his own household." Matthew 10:34-36.

Discomforting words. Unsettling. Many can't take them literally. They gloss them over with symbolism or bury them beneath reassuring platitudes. Few like to be at variance with anyone, let alone their own family. Most churchgoers have an image of Christianity that is too small to accommodate such a traumatic possibility.

Through the years countless little booklets have been prepared listing many of the promises of the Lord. Innumerable comforting sermons have been preached about the beautiful and reassuring promises that Jesus made. Strange, that these have so often ignored one of the promises that the Master made a special point to emphasize: Becoming a follower of His amounted to an automatic guarantee of getting into difficulty with other people.

If you think that because you are a Christian, because you are trying to serve God, that you will usually be well-treated, respected, appreciated, and approved, you are mistaken.

"Jesus promised His disciples three things," one writer has candidly said: "that they would be entirely fearless, absurdly happy, and that they would get into trouble."

Christ went about doing good and good only. He was perfect in kindness, sympathy, and love in His relationships with all. Yet He involved Himself in more trouble and conflict than anyone in the world before or since. Jesus, the Prince of Peace, was a storm center.

Even in His early years, first-hand experience introduced Him to the painful perplexity of "variance" with His own father and mother. Doing the appointed will of God as He set out to be about His Father's business conflicted immediately with His own parents' plans for Him and put Him at direct odds with them. He was compelled to give them a rebuke, a not altogether easy thing for someone as sensitive as He to do.

No one has ever been more misunderstood than Jesus Christ. No one has ever been more misrepresented. No one more mistreated.

It seems incomprehensible that living a life of total love should cause one to be shunned and scorned and even hated. But it does. It did for Jesus, and *it is absolutely essential that we come to understand right now that, to the extent you and I attempt to live God's love in this world, it will surely do it for us too.*

Through the centuries the honest words come ringing down, "If the world hate you, ye know that it hated me before it hated you." "Remember the word that I said unto you, The servant is not greater than his lord. If they have persecuted me, they will also persecute you." John 15:18, 20.

Loving is not easy. It costs. If you are not paying some of the price for it, you are really not doing it.

The Bible says, "All that will live godly in Christ Jesus shall suffer persecution." 2 Timothy 3:12. If you take the Bible just as it reads, then you will understand that this means just what it says: If you are *not*

81

encountering some form of persecution and trial, maybe you are *not* really living as a Christian!

If your life is comfortable and unruffled, if you enjoy approval, appreciation, and applause of nearly everyone, then something is seriously wrong with you spiritually. You may even be in danger of losing eternal life. It is a certainty that you are not daring to live God's love to the fullest extent right now.

No wonder Jesus said, "Blessed are ye, when men shall hate you, and when they shall separate you from their company, and shall reproach you." Then He gave the pointed warning, "Woe unto you, when all men shall speak well of you!" Luke 6:22, 26.

The lack of opposition is a sure sign that we are not daring to do anything at all significant for God.

The church may be finding almost universal favor because the public relations secretaries see to it that the church receives only a "good press." Because men praise the church for its good humanitarian works and the caliber of its institutions is no cause for us to rejoice and feel that we must certainly be totally doing the will of God. Let's not become smug and exclaim, "My! Isn't it wonderful how the Lord is blessing us!" Rather, achieving a wide degree of acceptance and popularity should prompt us to serious self-evaluation.

Why do the fires of persecution that once burned so fiercely, now appear dampened down? Could it be that the church has conformed to the worldly standards and therefore stirs up no opposition? Could it be that popular religion is not the kind that marked the primitive Christian church? Could it be that compromise with sin has dulled the "sword" of Christ? Are the great truths of the Bible so lightly treated that there is now little living godliness in the church? Could it be that this is the reason Christianity is apparently so popular? Could it be that if a revival of the faith and power of the early church were to shine forth the spirit of persecution would be revived and the fires of persecution would be rekindled?

For us to understand the potential for conflict inherent in Christianity, we must see its true revolutionary force. Though many would rather ignore such a drastic term, genuine Christianity is in fact a radical thing!

Christianity takes a person's natural sense of values and turns them upside down. It cuts his interests, his motives, his goals, his hopes, and his dreams—all that is essential to his existence—at cross-purposes with those of his neighbor or even his own family.

A Christian pledges his highest allegiance to the heavenly kingdom while other people give theirs to an earthly. Jesus rules supreme in the life of a Christian, while for anyone else self asserts and exalts itself—no matter how moral or proper or humane or religious they may appear to be.

A Christian sees the world through a different pair of glasses—corrective lenses. To a disciple of Christ, his car is not even his own, nor are his golf clubs or his hands or his stomach. To a non-Christian this is absurdity.

A Christian is compassionate in a world that considers compassion to be weakness. A Christian is honest in a world that is daily becoming more deeply programmed in dishonesty. A Christian is pure in a world that delights in wallowing in its own filth.

Surrounded by those dedicated only to their own self-interest, the Christian dedicates himself to the best good of others.

At a time when conventional wisdom throughout the land declares that there are no moral certainties or absolutes but that all things are relative, the Christian continues to believe in the concrete concepts of truth and error, darkness and light, morality and immorality.

A Christian insists that "sin" is no out-dated concept but still humanity's basic problem. A Christian does not need the world's approval or even his life if he must choose between that and compromising his convictions. Obeying God's law and doing God's will becomes more important to the Christian than life itself. Not because the Christian is stubborn. Not because he thinks himself right and everyone else wrong. But because *the Christian loves his God.*

The Christian martyrs of the past did not die for a truth, or a concept, or a standard, or a belief, or a church. They died for a Person.

They could dare to die because they dared to love. Him. Uncompromisingly.

Anyone who loves God that much is indeed a stranger in this world. If a person persists in such a revolutionary concept, though no matter how contrary to his nature and desire his conflict is, he will soon find himself surrounded by it.

"In a world of fugitives," T. S. Eliot said, "he who takes the opposite direction will appear to run away."

Anyone who lives contrary to popular philosophies, concepts, and traditions is destined for difficulty.

"God does not guide me," Martin Luther once wrote;

"He pushed me forward; He carries me away. I am not the master of myself. I desire to live in repose, but I am thrown into the midst of tumults and revolutions."

If you defend God's honor and keep to the truth no matter the cost, you will find yourself in trouble. Jesus did. If you yield and fail to condemn wrong and under pressure keep silent when your influence is needed to defend the right against wrong, you will avoid a lot of trouble. But you will also pay a terrible price, maybe the ultimate one, your own soul.

A subtle lethargy, spawned by ease, detracts many from fully grasping the shocking, staggering truth—a great controversy is raging in the world. Their comfortable, unthreatening life-style often denies the fact that the forces of good and evil are right now engaged in a frantic struggle for supremacy on the earth.

We Christians must come to understand that we are now to be living under *battle conditions.* Our choice of Christ as Captain of our lives enlists us in nothing short of total, all-out war.

Satan calls up all his evil allies and throws everything he has into the battle. Why does he meet so little resistance? Why do Christ's troops sleep?

The reason is that they are not close to their General. They don't share much of His Spirit. They don't feel repulsed by the enemy. They don't abhor his ways. They do not meet evil, as did Christ, with decisive and determined resistance. They do not realize the hideously evil power of Satan. They can't see the virulent nature of this foe of the universe. They don't hate evil, because they are ignorant of its power, malice, and vast extent.

Because of this ignorant and inexcusable delusion, the

forces of evil are now gaining ground at a pace that would alarm us if we could see it as it really is. Iniquity abounds, and, as the Bible predicts, the love of many is getting colder.

God needs men who will dare to love now. Dare to love in the face of hate and immense evil. Dare to love Jesus. Dare to love themselves as sons and daughters of God. Dare to love the unlovely. Dare to love their enemies. Dare to love though it may cost them their popularity. Dare to love though it may cost them their lives.

In this intense conflict the Christian's best weapon is love. Without it we are defenseless and can accomplish nothing. Unless our hearts are fired with love, our inert lives will slip one day over the brink of an empty eternity—without ever having seen action for God. Our apathy and indifference, our failure to become personally and vulnerably involved in the great controversy, will eventually cause us—by default—to lose all.

But if we choose to live God's love in this warring world, we will find ourselves inevitably at the battle front in the thickest action. We will be open to repeated, concentrated, furious attack by the fiercest, most cunning and cruel enemy the universe has ever known. We who have made a fetish out of our comfortable security will learn abruptly what it means to have "not peace, but the sword." We, like the irrepressible Martin Luther, will be thrown into tumult, revolution, and conflict. This is inevitable.

Just as bright light expels darkness, so truth expels error. The two cannot harmonize. To love and champion one is to hate and war against the other.

When Christians totally identify on the side of Christ and His love, trouble will come. Tension will develop between the Christian and the lovers of darkness. Violent spiritual war will break out. Opponents will rise—perhaps in our places of employment, our neighborhoods, even our own homes or churches. This will happen because all-out, revolutionary, love-filled Christian lives rebuke without fail those who reject the gospel. And especially those who profess to accept Christ but in the crunch prove otherwise.

Slumbering consciences resent such an uncomfortable disturbance. Comfortable religionists have always been irritated by Christians who cannot feel content with the status-quo world or church. Those who have chosen complacency, sleep through the building of the siege of works of evil, prejudice, hate, immorality, and selfishness. They squirm at being roused from anesthetic stupor. They recoil at any challenge to face a confrontation that could prove to be extremely costly.

On the other hand, God's true soldiers, His reformers —the Elijahs, Jeremiahs, Stephens, Pauls, Martin Luthers —have always been regarded as irritating, presumptuous troublemakers.

"And it came to pass, when Ahab saw Elijah, that Ahab said unto him, Art thou he that troubleth Israel?" 1 Kings 18:17. Here, in the sort of turn-of-the-tables that Satan loves to mastermind, the degenerate king of God's chosen, yet largely apostate, nation, charges one devoted totally to the will of God as being the source of difficulty, dissension, and upset for God's people. Exquisite irony!

Yet this pattern repeats over and over again and will

certainly continue to do so until the conflict between good and evil is at last ended. And if you are a Christian, you can expect it to happen to you.

We must understand that such trouble does not necessarily mean that something is wrong with our relationship with God. We must understand the Biblical theology of persecution for righteousness' sake. We must be able to recognize it as a natural part of the life lived in love in a world increasingly actuated by the opposite principle. A world strangely unwilling to accept love.

Even God's love.

Even when as expressed in the person of His very own Son, Jesus Christ the Crucified.

If a Christian fails at loving when he encounters opposition, he thus also fails to bear the fruit of victory in the cause of Christ. If this happens, all of the best intentions, all of the soundest beliefs, mean nothing.

As you pursue love, you reach the ultimate conclusion that genuine love, agapē, is not weak but powerful. Far from being some mild, pleasant, comfortable thing enjoyed at inclination—like a relaxing hobby or a flower garden—loving instead is an arduous, difficult, even hazardous full-time occupation. It is more like attempting to move a mountain with your bare hands. *Loving people is the hardest work in the world.* It can even seem to be the most discouraging, the most futile. But if you are a Christian, you will choose it. Regardless of the consequences as did Jesus.

"Let us not be weary in well doing," the Bible encourages, "for in due season we shall reap, if we faint not." Galatians 6:9. Claim this promise. And go on loving.

A healthy understanding of the principles of love will enable you to actually rejoice in troubles and conflicts. These can even be taken as a sign that God is definitely using you to do something significant for Him. Otherwise you would not be facing opposition!

"Blessed are they which are persecuted for righteousness' sake," Jesus said, "for their's is the kingdom of heaven. Blessed are ye, when men shall revile you, and persecute you, and shall say all manner of evil against you falsely, for my sake. Rejoice, and be exceeding glad: for great is your reward in heaven: for so persecuted they the prophets which were before you." Matthew 5:10-12.

Be glad for some persecution, counsels the Word! For a true believer it signals the depth of your commitment and proof of your actual engagement in God's campaign to win planet Earth!

Too many of us fear to rejoice in opposition and persecution. Someone may label us masochistic or paranoid! This did not worry Paul.

"Therefore I take *pleasure* in infirmities, in reproaches, in necessities, in persecutions, in distresses for Christ's sake," he said, "for when I am weak, then am I strong." 2 Corinthians 12:10.

We need to better understand the fact that conflict constitutes a natural part of strategic advancement for the cause of God. Progress of any sort always comes in the face of opposition.

"All those who have carried civilization forward have been angry men," once commented the much-loved preacher Peter Marshall, "grousing in the public parks, and the market places, nailing denunciations up on public buildings. They knew they were in a conflict and they took the wrongs in society—yes, and the wrongs in the church, terribly to heart."—John Doe Disciple, page 105.

In order to fulfill his destiny for God, the time comes when everyone must brave the judgment of others. Perhaps even that of his parents, his friends, his fellow-church-members, or his religious authorities.

"Christianity badly needs rash men," H. L. Shepperd has written, "who will not flinch from the crispness of religion, nor fear the result of stirring up wasps' nests."

A man who knew first hand the immense cost of daring greatly for God was Martin Luther. "Peace if possible," he wrote, "but truth at any price!"

"Never, for the sake of peace and quiet," echoed Dag Hammarskjold, "deny your own experience or convictions."

The Bible portrays the first followers of Christ as finally growing into lovers unafraid to live sacrificially for Him. Determined not to let their lives pass fruitlessly, they persistently faced Satan's challenges, obstacles, and attacks as they encompassed a pagan world with the love of God. Rather than accepting and reflecting its status quo, they "turned the world upside down." Acts 17:6.

Today the Father yearns to empower His children in the same way. With the same sort of conscientious courage and holy boldness. He is waiting for His people to step onto the stage of history. To press to the front of the ranks. To love for Him now. Totally, as Jesus did.

In spite of consequences.

Regardless of cost.

11

LOVE IS HANDLING YOUR HOSTILITY WELL

"If a man say, I love God, and hateth his brother, he is a liar: for he that loveth not his brother whom he hath seen, how can he love God whom he hath not seen? And this commandment have we from him, That he who loveth God love his brother also." 1 John 4:20, 21.

Two men once worshipped regularly in the same church. Both were conscientious craftsmen in the same trade. Both believed that the thoroughness of their work witnessed to their Christianity. And in their business practices both were scrupulously honest.

One day they both bid on the same small job. Only one, of course, got the contract. The losing bidder's wife was keenly disappointed. She had been depending on its profits to pay for the purchase of something especially nice she had been wanting for a long time. When the bids were made public, a significant difference appeared between the offers the two men had submitted. The disappointed wife concluded that the fellow-church-member-competitor must have purposely cut his bid extra low on the contract in order to keep her husband from it. This she suggested to her husband.

Unknown to her, however, the man had bid somewhat lower than usual because he, in fact, had wanted to use that particular job as a supervised training opportunity for his son who was learning the trade. The woman's presumptuous words had more than a passing effect on her husband. Dwelling on them, he eventually became convinced they were true.

The next week in church, without explanation, he abruptly refused to join in collecting the offering with his fellow craftsman. This was right, he believed, since he felt the way he did. Taking part with the other person as usual, he reasoned, would indicate that he countenanced his brother's lack of integrity. This, he decided, he could not conscientiously do.

The other deacon soon became aware of the hostility. Puzzled and hurt, he reacted by avoiding his fellow believer. He did not want to risk, he reasoned, doing anything that would further provoke his brother.

Each began to make a point of not being in the church lobby together. Members of the same Bible-study class, both felt relief when one chose to move to another group. They found themselves sitting with their families on opposite sides of the church during the worship service. People no longer saw them shaking hands together outside after the service as they had done for years.

Other church members became aware. Friends observed quickly and took sides.

Sensing that something serious was happening and noting the two men's declining spiritual interest, their pastor visited one of them one evening. While the pastor

92

was there, the other man, who lived close by, drove past and saw the preacher's car in the driveway. He immediately concluded that the pastor was taking that person's side. Hastily returning home, he at once wrote a letter to the president of the church's local conference. He asserted that the pastor was playing favorites among his members, was countenancing lack of integrity among the congregation's leaders, and was going to split the church.

The concerned president, who had never known of any difficulty in that church before, called the pastor on the phone and told him of the complaint. He suggested that the minister might be more cautious in how he dealt with some of his people.

The pastor, who wanted to please his conference president, was upset. He felt he had only been trying to be fair to the two men who were now clearly and openly at odds with each other. As a result, the pastor lost some of his enthusiasm for working with that congregation and began spending more time with another congregation in his district. He would be more discreet, he reasoned, to remain clear of the issue between the two men and thus not provoke more controversy.

Attendance at the weekly prayer meeting in the beleaguered church began to dwindle. When the time for election of church officers arrived, few members responded to the nominating committee's request to serve in leadership positions.

The pastor had previously scheduled evangelistic meetings in that town that winter. After evaluating the situation, however, he decided against it. One reason was the serious slump in the church's financial condition. The treasurer found difficulty keeping even the utility and maintenance expenses paid.

Members became reluctant to invite visitors to worship anymore. Some mentioned their fear that the visitors might sense the noticeable coldness and indifference. No baptisms occurred that year. Love had broken down.

The ability of an entire church congregation to express God's love to its community had been almost totally negated. And the growth of many spiritual lives had been stunted or destroyed. All because of one needless misunderstanding that spread like a cancer.

The church of Christ needs not to fear the opposition of the world so much as the evil cherished in the hearts of believers. This causes the most disastrous setbacks to God's cause. Jealousy, resentment, dark suppositions, hostility, and contempt do as much to destroy spirituality as anything else—no matter how evil.

Jesus pointedly warned Christians not to fear danger to the body, but rather danger to the soul, the spiritual side of a person. Nothing destroys the spirituality of persons, families, or churches more completely than does animosity.

"If a man say, I love God, and hateth his brother," the apostle wrote, "he is a liar: for he that loveth not his brother whom he hath seen, how can he love God whom he hath not seen? And this commandment have we from him, That he who loveth God love his brother also." 1 John 4:20, 21.

Our love for God is intimately and inexorably bound up with our love for people. It is not possible to have two mutually exclusive dimensions of our love, one for God and one for other human beings. You cannot love

God without also loving people. Neither can you truly love people without also loving God.

More than we realize, our love for people directly reflects our love for God. Even the redeemed at the last judgment will not fully grasp this principle. Jesus underscored this when He spoke of the amazement His own true followers will express when He reveals the love they actively showed to those in need. Love to those in need He regards as love expressed directly to Himself. "Inasmuch as ye have done it unto one of the least of these my brethren, ye have done it unto me." Matthew 25:40.

The quality of your love for people indicates and reveals the quality of your love for God. John, who experienced a great depth of love, wrote, "If we love one another, God dwelleth in us, and his love is perfected in us." 1 John 4:12. In God's estimation perfection is loving perfectly—loving to the best of our ability at any given moment in the course of our development into the character and image of Jesus Christ.

Only the person who unselfishly loves his brother truly loves God. The kind of spirit we show others demonstrates the kind of spirit we have in God's view.

"Whoso mocketh the poor reproacheth his Maker." Proverbs 17:5. "He that despiseth his neighbor sinneth." Proverbs 14:21. If you have offended a friend, you should realize your wrong. Then you should ask God to forgive, because your friend belongs to God. By offending him, you have offended his Creator and Redeemer.

A pious pretense of love for God cannot make up for the lack of love toward another person. Even an aggravating or sinful person who has deeply hurt you.

95

God asks you as a Christian to make His love tangible by loving every individual, including those you tend to dislike or disagree with.

People are like naughty little children. They need love most when they deserve it least. God wants those who claim Him to give this sort of costly love in the face of wrong, hurt, and anger. This is vitally important for the Christian himself, as well as for the one loved.

To let irritation and hostility toward another individual, however slight, eat away some of the love we have for that person is to tear down part of the foundation of our love for God Himself. Irritation, resentment, or anger toward another person cannot be ignored or repressed in a Christian's life. It is absolutely essential that it be handled and handled well.

"Let not the sun go down upon your wrath," Paul counseled. Ephesians 4:26. He clearly understood hostility's potential to destroy a relationship with God. He also advised, "Let all bitterness, and wrath, and anger, and clamour, and evil speaking, be put away from you, with all malice." Ephesians 4:31.

An expert at living God's love in the world must become an expert at handling his hostility well. This is necessary for living in the kingdom of God here and now, and for entering into the kingdom to come.

When Jesus Christ returns, He will not in some phenomenally supernatural way suddenly bestow on Christians the ability to relate well to people. Instead He will return to announce to the universe that some of His children have learned to love—to love enough to cope Christlike with personality conflicts, personal dislikes, and disagreements. Christ will come to declare them ready to be trusted with the kingdom of heaven.

For a Christian to handle hostility he must first understand and experience forgiveness. To handle irritation, resentment, and anger successfully and constructively you must yourself hang on the cross-shaped structure of forgiveness.

Forgiveness cannot be limited to an action at a certain point in time. You don't just conjure it up when you especially need it to meet a crisis someone else has precipitated. Forgiveness is not static. It is dynamic. It is a way of life. True Christians live forgivingly all the time. Just as God does.

If God's forgiveness is continually present, continually available, why not ours also? Forgiveness is a part of God—like tenderness, mercy, justice, and love. Forgiveness must be an unfailing part of a Christian, an attitude lived at all times. Just as he lives in love.

God is willing to give His forgiveness to anyone at any time, just as he is. His forgiveness is always there. When a man comes to God, he will find Him in a forgiving frame of mind. God even offers people forgiveness before they apologize. Of course they cannot appropriate His forgiveness for themselves until they repent. But that does not mean that it is not being constantly offered. Freely offered forgiveness leads a person to repent.

Too often you and I make our forgiveness conditional upon first receiving an indication of sorrow and apology. Then we willingly dispense it. But only if the asker is repentant enough to satisfy us. And only in proportion to the quantity of the apology offered.

God's example reminds us that we need to live so much in an attitude of forgiveness that we will have

97

forgiven people *before* they have wronged us. Thus our Father provided for the forgiveness of our sins before we committed them. This is better than forgiving people after they have wronged us. And it is much better than struggling to forgive them after they have at last apologized.

Only those who live forgivingly, the Bible says, are themselves forgiven. "And when ye stand praying, *forgive,* if ye have ought against any: that your Father also which is in heaven may forgive you your trespasses. But if ye do not forgive, neither will your Father which is in heaven forgive your trespasses." Mark 11:25, 26.

"Let all bitterness, and wrath, and anger, and clamour, and evil speaking, be put away from you, with all malice: and be ye kind one to another, tenderhearted, forgiving one another, even as God for Christ's sake hath forgiven you." Ephesians 4:31, 32.

God's constantly available, ungrudgingly given, total forgiveness extended unhesitatingly to you and me creates a penetrating warmth which evaporates our hostility toward others. This is the cleansing phase of God's love.

We Christians often speak about the value and beauty of God's forgiveness of sin. Yet we, who talk so glibly about it, often fail to give it content. Unfortunately the poor quality of our forgiveness creates a gigantic credibility gap in the minds of those who need to witness and experience the genuine article most. People today desperately need not only to see "love with skin on it" but forgiveness "with skin on it" too. Many will have to experience our sincere human forgiveness before they will venture to trust God's.

Says the Father, "I, even I, am he that blotteth out thy transgressions for mine own sake, and will not remember thy sins." Isaiah 43:25. From this we see that an important part of forgiving is forgetting. A Christian's forgiveness should be just as complete as God's.

Forgiving, Eileen Guder has suggested, is terribly costly. It means the one who forgives must give up all his "rights." In cases we do not feel forgiveness is warranted, we often feel no compulsion to forgive. Our "rights," we assert, have been violated. Realize, though, if you will, that a Christian has no such "rights." No dead man does, and Christians are people who are dead to themselves. God in His supreme purity and innocence has been wronged most of all. He has more "right" to retaliate, to withhold forgiveness, than anyone. Instead He keeps right on neglecting His "rights" and insistently offering total forgiveness. Even to those who hurt Him the worst. Can you and I, then, assert our "rights" and refuse to forgive on the ground that our "rights" have been violated?

As with all other spiritual dynamics, forgiveness involves the will more basically than the emotions. A Christian can successfully forgive someone while not feeling at all like doing it. He can choose to forgive and persist in that choice. Divine reinforcement is available. Genuine forgiveness comes best in answer to prayer. We cannot forgive of ourselves. This is just as impossible for us of ourselves as earning our own salvation. As impossible as loving the unlovely through our own power of the will. Or as loving our own selves by willing to do so. Christians are totally dependent upon God to give them the gift of forgiving others.

Jesus' followers pray for those who use them despitefully. His disciples find prayer to be the lance of bitterness. It drains dramatically the poison of hateful hostility from the human system. By purposely making the person who has wronged us the object of personal, pointed prayer, we take the first step in loving him. Love is not basically a feeling; rather it is a conscious choice to say or do that which is for the best good of another. Praying for someone is love in essence. When we do it, God can work a miracle not only in the other person's life but in ours as well. He can melt our most intense animosity and revengefulness with the warmth of His infused compassion right down to the place that is usually slowest to thaw—our level of feeling. Miraculously, then, our choice to be forgiving, and the act of God in making our forgiveness real, will be eventually accompanied by feelings of forgiveness.

That the Father will go to such lengths shows how intensely He cares about the quality of our human relationships. He marvelously enables us to keep these relationships open and unrestricted channels through which to express His own love to people.

As love flourishes best in a personal relationship, so also does forgiveness. "To know him is to love him," the expression goes. The better we know a person, the better we understand his motives and actions, and the better we can forgive his faults and failures—even his deliberate wrongs against us. The Bible says the reason Jesus qualifies so splendidly as our High Priest and is so able to forgive us is that He has experienced our *humanity*. In order to forgive us the Son of God actually became a man. He identified Himself with our interests and needs.

He was one with God; yet He linked Himself to us with ties that will never be broken.

This total identification with fallen humanity makes real God's unfailing forgiveness to us, extended undeservedly to you and me. The Father chose this intimate involvement with the human race in order to make real His offer of forgiveness to us. So we also must not shrink back from knowing and empathizing with our fellow mortals to make real our offer of forgiveness to others.

Many of our tensions, irritations, and aggravations result from misunderstandings with people. We could eliminate most of these if we would persistently and patiently try by God's grace to understand them. "If we could read the secret history of our enemies," says Henry Wadsworth Longfellow in his *Driftwood,* "we should find in each man's life sorrow and suffering enough to disarm all hostility."

Through His compassionate understanding of even His tormentors, Jesus could pray, "Father, forgive them; for they know not what they do." In the same way, thoughtful insight into what may be the traumatic and tragic life of someone who has hurt or wronged us can greatly help us to extend him our forgiveness.

12

LOVE IS GIVING HEALING CORRECTION

"Speaking the truth in love." Ephesians 4:15.

Consider this physician: He unmistakably diagnoses a serious, life-threatening disease in one of his patients. This disorder could be corrected only by immediate surgery. Yet, instead of promptly performing the operation, he sends his patient off for a relaxing vacation in Florida, instructing the sufferer to get plenty of rest and to enjoy the warm sunshine. Further, what would you think of that doctor if you knew that the relatively minor risks involved in the surgery and the probable discomforts of recuperation prompted the doctor's counsel?

With abhorrence would both the medical profession and the public regard such a physician. Yet you and I may be doing the same thing on the emotional-spiritual level.

Jesus came to this world announcing, "The kingdom of God is at hand." Matthew 3:2. Someone has dared to be so practical as to suggest that the kingdom of God is the kingdom of right relationships. Jesus came to set human persons right with God. Christians easily recognize the importance that such a program has for sinners. But Jesus also came to set human persons right with each other. The importance of this Christians tend often to overlook.

The Bible specifically points out that sin is anything that separates a person from God. And sin also separates one person from another.

Jesus stressed that sin against either God or a fellow human is a spiritual disease that must be dealt with and treated. He often expressed His concern that His disciples become experts not only at getting along well with God, but also with other people. In fact, the entire New Testament stresses the wrongfulness of sins of the spirit that destroy relationships among people more than such "gross" sins of the flesh as adultery and drunkenness. Yet we still show greater horror and severity toward the sins of the flesh than toward those of the spirit. Pride, animosity, and self-righteousness we tend to ignore or dismiss.

Strange that Paul should list such attitudes together with the others: "Now the works of the flesh are manifest, which are these; Adultery, fornication, uncleanness, lasciviousness, idolatry, witchcraft, hatred, variance, emulations, wrath, strife, seditions, heresies, envyings, murders, drunkenness, revelings, and such like: of the which I tell you before, as I have also told you in time past, that they which do such things shall not inherit the kingdom of God." Galatians 5:19-21.

In her book *To Live in Love* Eileen Guder suggests that the horror some church members profess against the sins of the flesh can actually be a way of calling attention away from more serious problems in their own lives. "Like Adam and Eve in the garden we are busy hiding our real nakedness—which is spiritual poverty before God. We are always erecting a spurious morality in order to conceal our inward immorality—not the obvious kind of pagan immorality, but the deeper immorality of self-centeredness and pride and impatience and irritation."—Page 107.

She suggests also that the church's toleration of a double standard for measuring sins—one for the sins of the flesh and a different one for the sins of the spirit (or attitude)—might be the biggest reason non-Christians think of most Christians as hypocrites. "They see, very clearly, our smug acceptance of the sins of attitude and temperament, our pretense that these things aren't really bad, worst of all that we often justify them in the name of Christian righteousness—a piece of sophistry which rightly earns the contempt of the world. We talk about the love of God and they laugh at us because they see so little of it in our lives."—Pages 108, 109.

How unfortunate that our human perspective on sin differs so radically from God's. He is more horrified by sins of temperament and attitude, for He knows how quickly and subtly they can wound and destroy relationships between people and between people and Himself. God in fact estimates everything only as it really is. We despise a drunkard. We tell him that his sin will ruin him eternally. Yet pride, selfishness, and covetousness we often leave unrebuked. But these sins God especially hates. They contradict His loving-kindness. They negate the unselfish atmosphere of sinless beings. For too long we have apathetically and purposely kept our eyes closed to sins of attitude and temperament.

As we have seen, forgiveness is the first principle in relating well to difficult persons. But there is another. Forgiveness and acceptance is not always sufficient. To bring healing and restoration to a relationship, another dimension is sometimes necessary.

Jesus' second great principle of human relations illustrates this additional dimension: "Moreover if thy brother shall trespass against thee, go and tell him his faults between thee and him alone." Matthew 18:15.

Someone can trespass against us not only by hurting us but also by injuring or wronging our church, our brother or sister, or our neighbor. We would not hesitate to take some action if we became aware that someone was planning to kill another person. This same sense of responsibility for others should carry over when, through sins of personality and temperament, someone hurts another. We have a duty, yes, even a command, to go and in love offer counsel and correction.

Jesus expects the wronged person to go to the one whom he feels is at fault and point it out privately. Unfortunately our typical reaction and response is just the opposite. Usually we insist that the "guilty" party come and offer an apology. We feel we have a "right" to expect this. Yet Christ teaches the startling concept that a Christian has no such "rights." Certainly no "right" to stop forgiving, accepting, and communicating because he is "right" and someone else is "wrong."

A Christian must live God's love in this world. This has priority. Nothing else matters. Not even his pride. The teaching of Jesus, that the wronged Christian must initiate the attempt to heal broken or strained relationships and must correct sins of attitude as well as of overt acts, reinforces this fact.

The natural man puts his desire to be thought well of by others and his desire to maintain a comfortable status quo in society ahead of any such risky and costly challenge. But those who sincerely follow the Man of Galilee soon learn this strange new priority. These are asked to do such seemingly illogical and unnatural things as surrendering to win, giving up to keep, and dying to live. To take the initial step, to go in love to someone who has seriously hurt or wronged you, with the pure purpose of lifting him up and building a closer relationship, requires you to surrender your pride, to give up your "rights," and to die to your own natural tendency for revenge. But what a superb way it is to handle your hostility! Nothing else squelches hostility more rapidly and efficiently than personally and directly confronting the individual who is its source. Nothing else builds a threatened relationship quite so quickly. Nothing else so thoroughly restores the channel through which God's love flows.

The first practical step in loving our enemies, he who "despitefully" uses us, is to forgive him. The second step in the divine order is to go to him with healing correction. Of course you always risk being rejected. Jesus realized that this would happen. He even gave guidelines to indicate what to do should this occur. See Matthew 18:15-17. Fortunately, the person who follows Christ's counsel can benefit from it whether his attempt at reconciliation is accepted or not. His action still fulfills a moral, ethical, and spiritual obligation and opportunity for ministry. It is the final dissolvant for persistent hostility. It also serves as a practical and observable demonstration of the reality of the wronged one's genuine desire to extend forgiveness. Those who wrong Christians need to see and experience more of *this* sort of "reprisal." It can serve to make God's love and forgiveness real to them.

Isn't this the sort of thing that Jesus by His life here was trying to show? God was terribly and innocently wronged by our world's selfishness and sin. Yet Jesus, representing the "innocent" wronged party, extended forgiveness and came to seek us out in our sinfulness, to confront us, to show us our wrong, to forgive us, and to offer the correction that would reveal to us a better way. God's wrath and hostility toward sin Jesus channeled into a ministry of love toward a rebellious world.

Over and over again this same pattern is to be reenacted by Christians as they confront evil and wrong today. In love we must go to those who have wronged either us or those for whom we are responsible, and freely offer forgiveness and healing. We may be often rejected, as Jesus was, but many will respond and through their experience will gain new dimensions in life both now and eternally. What a ministry this is for deeply touching lives with God's love and concern!

Yet most of us shy away. We feel exposed and vulnerable. We tend to handle our anger and give "correction" in an unbiblical but very human way. When someone wrongs us, we tend to try to "just forget it." This, we assume, is more virtuous. We think that "overlooking" a wrong is preferable to dealing with it. At times it may be. At other times it may not. It is unloving and cowardly to ignore a wrong that multiplies wrongs. At times silence may be golden, so the saying goes, but at other times it is just plain yellow.

We may lack the courage to risk bettering a relationship. Or we may not care that much. Or worse yet, we may harbor so many negative feelings ourselves that in spite of our attempts to forgive we may feel we cannot relate to the offending person in any way.

Yet trying to repress our animosities and hostilities toward another is not the Christian way of living with human relationships. These we must eliminate lest they destroy us.

"The typical sickness of this generation is neurosis," says George Vandeman in *Happiness Wall to Wall*. "Many doctors agree that half their patients suffer from it. . . . What is neurosis? Simply speaking, a person is neurotic when he represses something without eliminating it."—Page 86.

Failure to rid oneself of hostility and anger causes both emotional and spiritual sickness. As we have seen, repressed hostility destroys relationships person-to-person and person-to-God.

God could have contained His wrath at the awfulness of sin on earth. He could have bottled up His disappointment and anger within Himself and refused to have anything to do with our sinful planet. But He would not have been God then. He would not have been most loving. He loved us enough to involve Himself with sinful people, to channel His indignation into constructive and corrective action in our behalf.

The person who does not deal with his hostility in the Biblical way will fail at living God's love. If he tries to bottle it up within himself, it will, like the leaven of the Pharisees, expand until it explodes in unhealthy and destructive ways. Ever since Cain bludgeoned the life from his brother, people have been venting their hostility destructively. Physical, emotional, and spiritual death have resulted. On a large scale we call this war.

Whenever these principles of Jesus are disregarded, someone is hurt. Not with club, gun, or poison. The average churchgoer prefers something more comfortable, more subtle. His way, often done subconsciously, is to speak depreciatingly about the person who has hurt him. Of course, talking critically about another person outside his presence has the advantage of keeping one out of the electric chair! And it is such a spontaneous and satisfying way of getting "even"! For us humans it comes as naturally as breathing. When faced for what it really is, though, running people down is not only the most common way of dealing with anger, it is also the most cowardly, unchristian, and dishonest.

The natural human alternative to murdering a person is to murder his reputation, his prestige, or his standing. "Death and life are in the power of the tongue," teaches the proverb. "The words of a talebearer are as wounds, and they go down into the innermost parts of the belly." Proverbs 18:21, 8.

On the other hand, to go to someone who you feel is in the wrong, and to help him see what you believe his error to be, can be a ministry for God. To go to someone else and to demean and devalue the person you believe in the wrong is one of the greatest crimes against God and man that you can commit, no matter how casually or "kindly" you do it.

William George Jordan has written, "There are pillows wet by sobs; there are noble hearts broken in the silence whence comes no cry of protest; there are gentle, sensitive natures seared and warped; there are old-time friends separated and walking their lonely way with hope dead and memory but a pang; there are cruel misunderstandings that make all life look dark—these are but few of all the sorrows that come from the crimes of the tongue."

To speak negatively of another is to judge him. Judging is for Christians no more than is killing, stealing, or adultery. "Judge not that ye be not judged" is a divine warning not to be dismissed. "Speak not evil one of another, brethren," James warns. "He that speaketh evil of his brother, and judgeth his brother, speaketh evil of the law, and judgeth the law: but if thou judge the law, thou art not a doer of the law, but a judge. . . . Who art thou that judgest another?" Matthew 7:1; James 4:11, 12.

While the evil resulting from the mishandling of our anger and hostility is a great tragedy, that which will be missed—"what might have been"—if Christ's principles are not followed will be an even greater tragedy. Mistakes and blunders inevitably will occur as Christians deal with each other and others. These, God will forgive, but repentance must be genuine and marked by a desire to do better. Yet, while God forgives such lapses and failures, He cannot make up for the good, the blessing, and the spiritual growth and healing that "might have been" had His people lived more in harmony with His principles.

The church today desperately needs a greater vision of the marvelous dimensions of love and fellowship awaiting those who will dare to live God's love by consistently and fearlessly following His instructions for developing creative relationships with other people.

Jesus' words give an insight into this. Think about it again: "Moreover if thy brother shall trespass against thee, go and tell him his fault between thee and him alone: *if he shall hear thee, thou hast gained thy brother*." Matthew 18:15.

Something about this honest confrontation builds relationships remarkably. Most mistakenly feel that such an approach would fail to strengthen friendships, that it would do more harm than good. Not so, says the Master. "If he shall hear thee," it will give you a real brother.

Long ago, the wise man wrote, "Reprove not a scorner, lest he hate thee: rebuke a wise man, and he will love thee." Proverbs 9:8. Could it be, that instead of resenting your approach, as you might imagine, the person who is honest in heart will deeply and eternally appreciate the fact that you were willing to put yourself on the line enough to surrender your pride, to risk hurt feelings, to deny yourself and your "rights," and to approach him in an effort to be helpful and healing?

When we go to someone as Jesus suggested, by our actions we say that we genuinely care about him. We effectively communicate our concern, for we demonstrate the lengths we are willing to go, the risks we are willing to take—in his behalf.

On the other hand, if we fail to go, we may reveal either that we have not truly forgiven that person or that we do not really care enough. Too often it is the latter. Indifference is the greatest enemy of relationships between person and person or between people and God.

A display of indifference demonstrates a clear lack of concern. If we do not care, we of course do not, cannot love. And we have already seen that the failure to choose to love and to care about God and people constitutes the very essence of sin.

Most Christians never seem to comprehend that God regards as a ministry of love their going to someone to offer loving correction. We tend rather to view this more as an extremely distasteful duty than as a ministry. Yet the Bible says, "For whom the Lord loveth he correcteth; even as a father the son in whom he delighteth." Proverbs 3:12.

We Christians traditionally visualize ourselves as "doing the work of the Lord" in the world. We feel comfortable with the familiar concepts—doing God's work by witnessing or preaching or teaching. Those who go "to the ends of the earth" as missionaries we laud as working for the Lord. We understand the value of working for people and for God by feeding the hungry, clothing the naked, or serving in a church office. However, if God "chastens those whom he loves" in order to help them grow spiritually, and if you and I are dedicated totally to doing the work of God, is it not conceivable that it may sometimes be our role in service to confront other persons in order to give them a perspective on the wrong in their life and in order to help them overcome it and to better do the will of God?

Strangely, we usually feel that "chastening and correcting" must certainly be a ministry that God himself can carry out in someone's life who needs it—without our assistance! We do not hesitate to talk, sometimes almost boastfully, about how God can use us in a ministry to "save" sinners. Yet when it comes to a ministry that may save a fellow believer from losing his eternal life, we tend to think that our help is beyond God's ability to use effectively! So—fearing possible negative consequences, criticism, failure, presumption, rejection—we hold back. And we fail to step into a ministry of corrective love.

We often forget that we encounter and surmount similar obstacles in our other more traditional ministries. We often forget that without the indwelling power of the Holy Spirit the other ministries, as much as this, are also doomed to futility and failure. We think, perhaps, that we can more readily attempt and more comfortably carry out the others—at least in form--without a full measure of the Spirit. We know that the presence of the Spirit is obviously essential to the success of this especially sensitive ministry. Could it be that our failure to involve ourselves in this ministry of correction demonstrates our lack of reliance on the Holy Spirit even in the other areas of the work we are struggling to do for God?

Although the terms "ministry of correction" or "constructive criticism" do not occur as such in the Bible, Scripture mentions this facet of Christian duty. Paul urged Timothy not only to do God's work by preaching the word, but also to "reprove, rebuke, exhort with all longsuffering and doctrine." 2 Timothy 4:2. He advised the Colossian Christians, "Let the word of Christ dwell in you richly in all wisdom; teaching and *admonishing* one another." Colossians 3:16.

How long has it been since a Christian brother has admonished you in love over one of your failings in

113

order to help you fit more perfectly into the will and work of God? If a brother did so attempt to admonish you, how would you react? Are you secure enough emotionally and spiritually to let another person frankly tell you what he considers your greatest weakness? Or what he sees in you that keeps you from becoming more Christlike? Or how he thinks you could be a better witness? Or how he thinks you could be a better Christian father or mother?

Do you see the great good such occasions could produce if done in genuine love and truly under the influence of the Holy Spirit?

In commercial flying, airline pilots undergo what the industry calls a proficiency check. The pilot is required periodically to demonstrate his ability with a competent check pilot by his side. The experienced instructor offers criticism and advice on how he can perform better and more safely. Pilots recognize such "check-rides" as a tremendous stimulus to greater proficiency and safety.

A spiritual "check-ride" administered by people who really care might not be such a bad idea for a Christian now and then. It might, if in love and under grace, improve his performance for God and other humans.

God used Aquila and Priscilla in a loving ministry of growth and correction for the best good of the eloquent preacher Apollos. Though Apollos was a "mighty man in the Scriptures," he nonetheless was giving a seriously inadequate exposition of the gospel to his listeners at Ephesus. Although Apollos had not actually wronged them, he did need new light. These two humble and untrained lay people, tentmakers by trade, did an important work for God by daring to take Apollos aside and tell him of a serious lack in his preaching.

The great preacher took the criticism well! And he experienced spiritual growth by it! This we learn from the way his preaching changed and increased the blessings of many. See Acts 18:24-28. From this we see that healing correction, like the circular ripples from a rock dropped in a placid pool, keeps spreading out and affecting many lives beyond the one first directly touched.

"Criticism offered under a sense of Spirit-led constraint and moral necessity is one of the most exacting and costly ministries there is," writes Kenneth S. Roundhill in *Christianity Today*, January 7, 1972, p. 8.

He also remarks how Paul's life provided so many moving examples of love in critical action which reveal how alive he was to the needs of others:

"He rebuked Peter publicly before the Antioch church for his momentary defection from the purity of the Gospel because it stemmed from fear of public opinion and had affected others. . . . It was a public defection calling for public rebuke. (Gal. 2:11-14.) That Peter bore no grudge is evident by his later remarks about Paul in his second letter. (2 Peter 3:15.) Mark felt the keen edge of Paul's moral distress when he failed Paul and his companions at Pamphylia (Acts 15:36-40); this rebuke may have had something to do with Mark's later becoming a very useful fellow worker. (2 Tim. 4:11.) Love that aims for the supreme good of another will on occasion cut in order to cure."

Without doubt this "cutting" Mr. Roundhill refers to holds many back from administering corrective Christian healing. This was true of the hypothetical physician mentioned earlier, who would avoid the corrective action of surgery for fear of causing his patient pain! We do not wish to cause hurt to another.

Even the intrepid Paul expressed his concern that the constructive criticism he was led to give by the Spirit might be too severe. After his letter to the Corinthians had been sent, Paul feared that he might have cut too deeply, when he wanted only to help. He feared that the Corinthian believers might be further alienated. At times he even wanted to recall his words. Paul knew that the church was divided; he encountered ingratitude and betrayal from those he had expected to show sympathy and support. He sensed the danger of congregations that condoned sin; therefore he felt the duty to show the Lord's disapproval of their sins. Nevertheless he feared that he might have been too severe.

The apostle went so far that he even shared with the Corinthians his inner conflict in his valiant attempt to help them grasp that he was acting out of a compulsion of love for them. His cry, echoing down through the years, is essentially that of every man who dares to step into this arena for God and to undertake the painful, almost torturous, ministry of offering healing correction. "For out of much affliction and anguish of heart I wrote unto you with many tears; not that ye should be grieved, but that ye might know the love which I have more abundantly unto you." 2 Corinthians 2:4.

While the great man of God weeps at the pain he knows will be inflicted, he persists courageously in his course, encouraged by the knowledge that the correction he offers at such great cost to himself will actually result in an abundant expression of healing love. Paul does what he has to do—in spite of the unpleasantness; in spite of the distastefulness—because he loves people enough to seek their best good. Regardless of the cost or the pain to themselves or himself.

You and I must also recognize the role of correction in expressing love. His correction was given "that ye might know the love which I have more abundantly unto you." We who wish to live God's love also need to see it in such full potential. When we do, there will be no more drawing back.

Yet, unlike the other ministries, it will never come to be a work that we approach joyfully. But we will recognize its necessity to spiritual growth for others and ourselves. The Bible both sympathizes and challenges when it says, "Now no chastening for the present seemeth to be joyous but grievous [to both the giver and the receiver]: nevertheless afterward it yieldeth the peaceable fruits of righteousness unto them which are exercised thereby." Hebrews 12:11.

Long ago God commanded a young man to offer revealing correction, not just to one other person but to a whole nation: "Cry aloud," He told Isaiah, "spare not, lift up thy voice like a trumpet, and shew my people their transgressions, and the house of Jacob their sins." Isaiah 58:1. The destiny of God's people, the destiny of God's plan for the world, was then at stake. It still is.

Children actually feel deprived if their parents do not correct them. Most youngsters flourish on loving discipline. It is a solid proof to a child—on the important level of the subconscious—that he is loved and cared about. Even teen-agers, we are told by the behavioral experts, want to be told when they make mistakes. They want their parents to correct them when they err, despite the fact that they may complain at the time.

Could it be that in the same way, many who err against their fellowmen or against themselves or against God, also actually want, at least subconsciously, to have someone care enough about them to offer them correction? Could it be that many sense that for them here is a means of betterment, of growth and healing?

Just as certainly as there is a ministry for the concerned Christian in comforting the afflicted, there is an equally valuable work for God in the world of afflicting the comfortable!

Jesus was of course a master at the ministry of correction. He would take a man's sin and, in dealing with it, turn that sin into a steppingstone toward the kindgom of heaven for that person. Lying, adultery, anger, pride, were all directly confronted by Him and that confrontation often led a man or a woman closer to God. Jesus encountered many thorns, but He always tried to turn every one of them into a crown!

Nicodemus, a man meticulously careful about his religion and his law-keeping, a renowned spiritual leader of impeccable moral character, felt the sword of the Spirit. Jesus dared to thrust on him the shocking realization that he knew not even the first step in the science of salvation!

Jesus confronted, also, the rich young ruler and, with a few well-chosen words aimed directly at his conscience, prompted the young man to face himself honestly for the first time. Christ's unmistakable challenge, if accepted, could have revolutionized his life. Unfortunately he rejected the correction. Note, however, that this rejection did not hinder Jesus from extending His message in love.

One might have expected the woman at the well to reject Him. He must have startled and embarrassed her, perhaps even more than He did the young ruler. In most circles His abrupt approach would be considered impudent. Yet in His remarkable sensitivity for people, Jesus sensed that this lonely and guilt-ridden woman was looking for something better. His to-the-point confrontation not only led to a dramatically changed life, but also to a full-scale revival in her city! Telling a woman that she is an adulteress is a rather unique way to initiate an evangelistic contact with an entire town. It is a profound way to demonstrate, however, the potential for miracles in the healing ministry of love.

The way that Jesus related to the Pharisees also teaches us. The face-to-face rebukes He unflinchingly handed them are some of the strongest and most penetrating anyone has ever given. Next to a pig nothing was quite so repugnant to a Jew as was a snake. Jesus did not hesitate, however, to categorize many of the religious leaders of His day as vipers. This was done right in the presence of their adherents. He also told them they were hypocrites who were rotten through and through inside. The only thing there is any record of Jesus writing in His entire lifetime was the sins of the Pharisees. These He drew clearly in the dust of a Jerusalem street with His own finger!

Shocked and angered by His pointed denunciations, some of them became frantic about securing His destruction. Others, temporarily filled with hurt and resentment, were nonetheless jolted in their entire being by His piercing words. Jesus jarred open their inner lives, enough in some cases for the Spirit to get in and do His work. And many of the Pharisees who had received such withering criticism from Jesus became His devoted followers after His ascension.

Through Christ's ministry of correction you and I may learn the principles vital in guiding our own attempts to bring healing, growth, and salvation to others in this way. If they are followed, these guidelines ensure that only good will eventually result from the occasions in which God calls us to touch the lives of others with admonitions.

The first rule drawn from the Master's life on giving healing correction is that we must understand clearly that the truth of God alone can make the offensive and do any cutting that is necessary—not the person presenting the truth. The truth only is sharp enough to pierce effectively. Anything else is too blunt and does too much damage. "For the word of God is quick, and powerful, and sharper than any twoedged sword, piercing even to the dividing asunder of soul and spirit, and of the joints and marrow, and is a discerner of the thoughts and intents of the heart." Hebrews 4:12.

This does not mean that we must search out and bombard the offending one with a string of Bible texts. It does mean that our message of loving correction of conduct or belief must be based soundly in the Word of God. We must bear only a message that the Bible plainly sets out. Otherwise, we have no business going. More often than not, confronting another person with our own opinions or conclusions or suggestions about them would simply be a pious way of expressing our hostility and our desire to see them change or conform to an image more acceptable to us, rather than to the Word. It is not our task to make people acceptable to us. It is our privilege to help others to grow in ways that will make them acceptable as citizens of the kingdom of heaven.

When the Bible refers to the ministry of correction, it shows it to be centered on the Word. "Let *the word* of Christ dwell in you richly in all wisdom; teaching and admonishing one another." Colossians 3:16. "Preach the word; be instant in season, out of season; reprove, rebuke, exhort with all longsuffering and doctrine." 2 Timothy 4:2. Nowhere does any justification exist for giving admonition and counsel to others beyond clear-cut Scriptural laws, principles, and guidelines.

The second rule drawn from the Master's life on giving healing correction is that without exception it be carried out only in genuine Christian love. It is all about "speaking the truth in love." Ephesians 4:15. Jesus unfailingly projected truth to people, even though it might hurt—an expression of God's love. Jesus suppressed no word of truth. But He always spoke the truth in love, with infinite tact, thoughtfulness, and kindness. He was never discourteous or disrespectful. He never *needlessly* spoke a hard or stern word. He never gave *needless* pain. He did not attack and condemn human weakness. He spoke only the truth. But He did so only in love. He exposed false piety, lack of faith, and wickedness. But as He spoke His most scathing rebukes, tears were in His voice.

Jesus challenges us to live God's love in the world as He did, gently yet forcefully—and only for the healing of others. Honesty without love, it has been said, is

121

brutality; and love without honesty is sentimentality. But Christians know that genuine love *involves* honesty and Christian honesty involves love. "Criticism, like rain," Frank Clark has written, "should be gentle enough to nourish a man's growth without destroying his roots."

The ability to combine truth and love successfully is, of course, humanly impossible. You and I can no more do it than we can earn our own salvation, love our own selves well, love the unlovely, or forgive the unforgivable. It is totally beyond our finite reach. Yet "it is not ye that speak, but the Spirit of your Father which speaketh in you." Matthew 10:20.

When we permit the Spirit to use us, when we are willing to take the risk of carrying out this important and delicate assignment for God, lives otherwise impenetrable can be opened to the righteousness of the Father and victories can be won for the kingdom of God that would otherwise never occur. The first pangs of hurt and anger that often accompany this work can be the pain of birth, the herald of new life, new birth in Christ! Love and truth will join to do their cutting. But it will be done only to bring healing and salvation.

Some speak in "love" but fear to speak the truth. Their words are meaningless. Others speak the "truth" but not in love. Their words destroy. But by the grace of God we can speak the truth in love.

And as we do, miracles happen.

13

LOVE IS CONFESSION

"Confess your faults one to another, and pray one for another, that ye may be healed." James 5:16.

Seated with my fellow students in the crowded chapel of the Pacific Garden Mission that muggy Chicago night I was thoroughly enjoying my attitude of pious pity toward down-and-outers in the room. Good Christian seminarians all, we displayed well scrubbed faces reflecting the glow of our growing ability to do exegesis in the book of John in Greek. Seated together in a row, suited and tied, shoes carefully polished, hair well combed, we exuded the aroma of after-shave and hair tonic.

Though I would probably not have admitted it, for fear of showing my lack of sophistication, I had never seen in one place before quite such a conglomerate of humanity as this hunch-shouldered group—people you seldom see but fit your mental picture when you read that Bible text about feeding the hungry and clothing the naked. Here they all were, winos, dopers, prostitutes, and just ordinary bums.

A plain-looking man up front in a creased and baggy

gray suit preached along in a hard-to-listen-to monotone. My mind drifted—from pointers I would have liked to give him on improved inflection, to wondering whether anyone had ever done any scholarly research on the attendance figures at mission chapel services in relation to the number that showed up in the dinner queue.

My musing was temporarily halted by an unexpected and almost startling rise in volume from the speaker. He was reading some texts he evidently wished to impress on his listeners. "All we like sheep have gone astray," he proclaimed. I glanced at my nearest classmate and raised an eyebrow. He nodded his head slightly as if agreeing with my unspoken thought that this was certainly an appropriate verse to use on a congregation like the one we were observing. "Might as well let them have it," I whispered to him. "The truth can't do them any harm."

"We have turned every one to his own way," the preacher went on, reinforcing my opinions about the human degradation that surrounded me.

"All have sinned, and come short of the glory of God." An appropriate text.

Then as the preacher lowered his volume and went into the application of his texts my mind drifted again.

After the sermon was over, our group briefly toured the mission facilities and started to leave. As we went out the door, one of my companions remarked, "We have been instructed that this sort of work is to be left to others."

"I'd say we are quite fortunate," I quickly responded. Other well-groomed heads nodded in agreement.

Arriving home late that evening, I entered with satisfaction the two hours "observation" time on my class report schedule. I completed another assignment and, after the long day, welcomed the chance to crawl at last into bed. But sleep did not come easily.

For some reason the words of that unimpressive mission preacher kept running through my mind. "All we like sheep have gone astray." "All have sinned, and come short—" I remembered the way his long glance had carried to the back row where we students were seated when he said, "Everyone in this room tonight is a sinner." I thought of how I had been amused by that and wondered why no one had told him that we were visiting seminarians. Finally I sank into a troubled sleep.

In the days that followed, the mission preacher's words kept forcing themselves into my conscious thoughts. They kept working their way determinedly through the accumulated layers of my ego until the time came when quite suddenly and inescapably I could no longer resist their impact. Finally they brought me face to face with a fact that I had never before admitted: I, Douglas Cooper, was a sinner.

The full weight of this startling insight bored a hole through my pride and self-sufficiency and allowed me to catch a glimpse of myself as I really am—sinful, selfish, proud, deceitful, hostile, unaccepting, unloving, and impatient.

In desperation and despair I was led at last to come before God with something that had been missing when I approached Him before—honesty. When I saw myself as I am, I was left with no alternatives. I could only confess my utter unrighteousness and wretchedness.

That has made all the difference. Before it happened, I had only half a need for Jesus. Theologically, of course, I knew better than to believe that my record of obedience to God's commandments, my harmony with the standards of the church, and my service rendered to God would earn me salvation.

But on the level of actual Christian experience I was letting these things stand as a barrier between Christ and me. I had assumed that because I was doing them I was quite a good fellow. It seemed that in some way my faithfulness should help me score a little higher with God than other people who were not being as faithful and conscientious as I.

God had to take me and rub my face in my own wretchedness a few times. Beginning with the words of that mission preacher, I finally got the message about the sort of person I am.

I know now that no matter how well I obey, how correctly I believe, or how sacrificially I serve, I will never be of myself in any way better than some other person—whether thief, prostitute, or alcoholic. The quite proper appearing clothing I was wearing around with a great deal of assurance turned out to be filthy rags after all. I have learned that, no matter how meticulously and painstakingly I attempt to dress myself up, in the penetrating eyes of God I am still a wretched sinner.

From then on I could only keep on confessing what I am and trusting in God's unexplainable fondness for me, a sinner. I know now that I need all the forgiveness I can get. I need it just as much as the "worst" person in the world. I need Jesus Christ as a Saviour just as much. I can only depend totally on Him as Redeemer, just as those people in the Pacific Garden Mission had to do. I saw that I could claim absolutely no spiritual superiority over them.

We Christians are simply not aware of the extent of our own sinfulness. We do not confess enough.

I remember also the first time I visited a meeting of Alcoholics Anonymous. A highly-respected leader in our community stood and introduced himself. I have never forgotten the shock. "I am Tom," he said. "I am an alcoholic."

Everything in me rebelled against his making such a statement. I wanted to shout out that he was no such thing. I wanted to tell the others there about his good character. I knew he had not taken a drink in years. And I wanted to tell him that he must not depreciate himself like that.

Tom went on. Calmly, he told the group he was able to maintain his sobriety only on a moment-by-moment, day-by-day basis, only as he kept his hand in the hand of divine power. He said that even after all the years of successfully battling alcohol he knew he could never trust himself, because he was and is and always will be by nature an alcoholic.

Afterward Tom explained to me that only by honestly admitting his weakness to other people who also were struggling with the problem could he and all those in AA maintain the victory in their personal battles against alcohol.

Since that time I have often been refreshed by the thought of the striking honesty clearly and sincerely present in that meeting. I felt a unique spirit of unity and fellowship present as men and women unashamedly faced their condition and their need together. Pride, egotism, and pretense evidently do not coexist well in the same atmosphere where statements like "I am an alcoholic" are made.

I knew many lives in our town had been changed by that group. I knew many of the people who, like Tom, were in it, not just for the help they could get for themselves, but also for others. Through their sharing, their honesty, and their concern they were reaching out their hands and helping fellow strugglers.

What would a church meeting be like if the pastor would stand up and say, "I am Tom. I am a sinner"?

Traditionally Christian worship includes singing, prayer, and preaching. Each is uniquely valuable. But have you ever attended a Christian gathering which set aside time and created the atmosphere for the confession of faults and sinfulness? If so, how many members would misplace their car keys just before time to leave for the service? Such a concept is not familiar or comfortable. Yet the Bible still reads, as it has for a good many centuries now, "Confess your faults one to another, and pray one for another, that ye may be healed." James 5:16.

Confession costs. It gets down to the nitty-gritty, to the level where pride and ego are really dug in, and compels you to die to yourself.

Confession hurts. It pulls endeared sins out piece by protesting piece.

But should it be so hard? Confession hurts the pride. But a dead person has no pride. And Christians are dead to themselves.

God has portrayed confession as a way of life for the Christian. He wants us living in an attitude of constant confession to Him and, where necessary, to others. This is the only way to appropriate His constantly available and constantly needed forgiveness. And, sinners that we are, we cannot do without this for a minute. God cannot forgive us unless we accept. And we cannot accept unless we confess.

Living in an attitude of constant confession is necessary to a love relationship with God. Likewise, it is necessary to our love relationships with other people. Just as our confession of wrongs to God appropriates His forgiveness, so our confession of wrongs to other people appropriates their forgiveness.

Your prayer of confession cannot be limited to repentance for stealing ten dollars when you were thirteen years old or for speaking a harsh word to a brother the day before yesterday. Important as these specifics are, in genuine confession you will have much more to say. You will have to recognize that by nature you are a sinner, tend always to sin, and can find righteousness only in total, moment-by-moment dependence on Christ.

So in our confession to one another the heart of the matter lies in a willingness to recognize the utter extent of our disease of sinfulness. With this in mind, confession takes on a new role in our worship and fellowship together. A Christian should not confess to fellow humans specific sinful acts unrelated to them which he has committed in the past. Their knowledge of this is of no value to them. It might conceivably do harm.

However, he should confess his selfish tendencies, his stifled conscience, his lack of love. He can thus seek

9—L.G.L.

release and support and freedom and victory from God in such confession. He can also make his deepest needs known and receive the healing therapy of the specific prayers of his fellow believers for him. This is God's concept of public confession within the circle of Christian fellowship.

In addition to confession to God alone and "public" confession within the Christian fellowship there is one-to-one confession. Jesus referred to this when He said, "Therefore if thou bring thy gift to the altar, and there rememberest that thy brother hath ought against thee; leave there thy gift before the altar, and go thy way; first be reconciled to thy brother, and then come and offer thy gift." Matthew 5:23, 24.

His point is that offerings to God are pointless unless we are right with all other people. God's appointed way for a Christian to get right with someone he may have wronged is by one-to-one confession. This restores and rebuilds relationships. This starts spiritual life flowing again.

God recognizes the spiritual value of confession so much that He has given it to us as a part of our worship. He does not give us an option—doing it or not doing it. Just as the Bible commands Christians to pray, to witness, to study the Word, it commands us to confess. "Confess your faults one to another, and pray one for another, that ye may be healed." Confession must be a part of our life if we are to receive the healing—spiritually, mentally, and physically—that is conditional upon its practice.

Could it be that one reason so little spiritual and emotional and even physical healing exists in the church today is that there is so little confession? Have we succeeded in creating an atmosphere within the church where openness and honesty are actually discouraged?

"Most men," Thoreau once wrote, "lead lives of quiet desperation." This is true for many people in today's world—both mentally and spiritually, both inside and outside the church. Unless we stop the pious playacting and start being honest about our true condition and needs, unless we start confessing our faults one to another and confronting them together as God has willed, few victories we will gain.

We need not tense up over the idea of confession. We need not think of it as some over-wrought, over-emotional, soul-pouring testimony of sordid events we will later regret mentioning.

There are three levels: The sins may be the kind that we should bring to God alone. They may be the kind that we should also confess to those we have wronged. Or they may be the kind of public offense that we should confess publicly.

If confession is kept on the appropriate level, it can be what God meant it to be, one of the most dynamic forces for the extension of love and healing. Confession creates the sort of atmosphere where the Holy Spirit can work in lives productively.

Some of the misunderstanding and hesitancy about confession may stem from the fact that on first appearance it is perhaps the one and only area of Christian life and experience where there is no direct example of Jesus to follow. We have Christ's example for praying, facing temptation, extending forgiveness, offering healing correction, and loving the unlovely. But not to confessing sin. Jesus never sinned. We can, however, follow the Master's example of honesty, openness, and freedom in admitting His needs and weaknesses. In this sense, then, though He was pure and sinless, Jesus Christ lived confessionally. How dare we, who are sinners, fail to live in an attitude of confession?

Jesus spoke freely of the almost overpowering temptations and pressures He had to face. On that awful night in the garden, with the burden of the whole world crushing down on Him, Christ confessed His frailty and vulnerability. His own sense of need came close to overwhelming Him. So strong was it that He pleaded for the support of His closest disciples. "And he took with him Peter and the two sons of Zebedee, and began to be sorrowful and very heavy. Then saith he unto them, My soul is exceeding sorrowful, even unto death: tarry ye here, and watch with me." Matthew 26:37, 38.

Jesus felt so fearful, so weak and insufficient for the immense challenge before Him, that in total honesty both to His followers and to God Himself He asked His Father to take the terrible burden from Him if possible so He would not have to bear it.

Jesus proved unforgettably that the dimensions of confession reach beyond admitting one's sins and mistakes to God or to another person or persons. His life revealed that the principle of confession includes a total honesty with God and with others about our weaknesses and need for dependence on God.

God hates pretense. Annanias and Sapphira pretended to be faithful members of the early Christian church. Apparently religious people, whose morals and integrity would probably never have been questioned by their fellow believers, they tried to cheat and rob God. They paid with their lives the price God required for pretending.

Jesus, grieved to His heart at the hypocrisy and gigantic living lies of the Pharisees, directed His most scathing rebukes their way and publicly exposed their inner corruptness. Yet He did so only in infinite love.

Christ in His Sermon on the Mount taught that no one who tries to appear what he is not, or whose words do not reveal his true feelings, is truthful. Everything a Christian does should be as transparent as sunlight.

Yet only by the grace of God can we live without pretending to be better or different from what we really are and live God's love significantly in the world.

One of the biggest challenges Jesus faced was getting men to admit the truth about themselves. With many He never succeeded. As a result, these people never confessed their sin. Sadly, they never came to recognize their need of Him as a Saviour. But with others He did succeed. And these became His followers.

How many today miss everything because they also fear the honest truth about themselves and their real needs?

How especially tragic to realize that the reason many hesitate is their intense desire to obtain the very thing they are missing—love and acceptance. For fear of being rejected when others are permitted to see them as they are, they trust no one, including God, with their real selves.

We Christians need to see our own self-righteousness and pretense for what it often really is—a misguided quest for love and acceptance. Most people want love so desperately that they will do almost anything to get it, including pretending to be something they are not or pretending to be better or more dedicated or kinder than they really are. They pretend to other people, God, and even themselves.

When you and I see through such facades in others, we should rely on God's grace so that we will not become simply irritated and try to point out the fraud. We should be instead so loving and so accepting that they will feel the freedom to be themselves.

You, as a Christian, enjoy an immense advantage in becoming open and honest. You have the assurance that God has accepted you just as you are. How easy it is, then, to be yourself to others too. This freedom to be yourself is one of the most refreshing gifts the Lord gives you. You don't need to "grandstand," to struggle to make others think you are something you aren't—because in Christ you are all you need to be.

A person who cannot confess the truth about himself is a hopeless slave, shackled by the burden of living a lie. No wonder the Bible says confession brings healing! When a person confesses to God, he experiences the release of God's love and forgiveness—he becomes truly free in a growing relationship with God. When a person can be honest with society about what he is and confess himself and his need, he has a solid foundation for healing and growth of relationships between people.

Freedom to be oneself is necessary to any relationship. Mutual confession, trust, and shared need draw people close to one another. A spirit of openness creates an atmosphere in which the Spirit of God can work to fuse lives to each other and to God. Confession has always been a part of revival, a part of any significant, life-changing Christian fellowship.

A law of human dynamics, a law established by the Creator Himself, is that Christian honesty and confession spontaneously generate love, closeness, unity, and fellowship. To fail at openness is to fail also at loving.

The apostle Paul is an example of a Christian leader whose life was open and transparent. Paul made no effort to hide his personal problems and weaknesses. Paul, the most educated of the New Testament writers, the best theologian, and the most effective missionary and evangelistic preacher, was humble and open enough to write in a letter to his young intern minister Timothy and confess to him "that Christ Jesus came into the world to save sinners; of whom I am chief"! 1 Timothy 1:15.

As the world witnesses the utter honesty of Christians with one another, many will be drawn toward this healing and refreshing fellowship. It is the sort of thing people are longing for today, both inside and outside the church. Many are tired of playing games. They want to be able to find an atmosphere where they can feel safe to be themselves openly.

Should the church not be a citadel for this sort of loving friendship? Should people go to bars or group therapy sessions in their efforts to get it? Should not the church, blessed with the fruits of the Holy Spirit in its midst, be the place? Should not the church be famous for its fellowship? Should it not be the beacon leading lost people out of darkness into light? Into the fellowship of Jesus Christ? Into the atmosphere of heaven on earth? Into that which alone can fill the empty hearts of the lonely?

Without attitudes of openness, brokenness, and confession, the church cannot draw sinners into its fellowship. It cannot evangelize.

Basic in revival, reformation, evangelism, witnessing, friendship, and fellowship, confession deserves a greater place in the church.

The Bible shows repeatedly that the greater a man is spiritually, the greater is his attitude of confession. We often find in Scripture the sins, mistakes, and weaknesses of the giants of the faith. We find their confessions to God, to their contemporaries, and to us. These failures are as clearly and forthrightly chronicled by the inspired pen as are their victories for God. Adam, Moses, David, Elijah, Jonah, Isaiah, John, Peter, Paul, and many others have left behind a record of their struggles. Out of their brokenness and confession springs spiritual healing and life for many.

14

LOVE IS FELLOWSHIP

"But if we walk in the light, as he is in the
light we have fellowship one with another."
1 John 1:7.

The success or failure of Christ's mission to our world
hinged on whether or not people would believe in Him
as the Son of God. If they would not, His life, His
ultimate sacrifice, and His resurrection would have been
in vain.

How did He go about establishing to a highly
skeptical world that He was the Christ come to save
mankind—with only three years to do it?

He formed a group fellowship of twelve individuals
who, except for Judas, lacked education and refinement
and who differed in interests and personalities. From our
human viewpoint we can hardly think of a less likely
method of accomplishing something of the magnitude of
the challenge Jesus undertook.

We might expect Him to have attempted to win
allegiance and prove His divinity by concentrating
entirely on the working of miracles. We find, however,
that He always performed His miracles to meet genuine
human needs, not to prove a point. Jesus knew that God

had been showing Israel miracles for centuries, only to have them persistently rebel at living in His will. Christ sensed that supernatural feats, no matter how much attention and applause they might attract, would not suffice to draw us to trust in Him as our eternal Saviour.

Jesus might have limited His ministry in the world to logical expositions of the truth about Himself. He could have been quite convincing with His logic and persuasive with His arguments. But Jesus knew that understanding the truth is not enough to change lives for heaven. The Godhead's final, all-out effort to bridge the gap to perishing humanity called for something more.

Yes, Christ would come in human flesh, work miracles, and teach truth. This would awaken interest and inform people of the eternal issues at stake. God determined not only to grip imaginations and intellects, but to capture hearts too.

How? By sending Jesus Christ to establish a fellowship of love in the world such as had never before been seen or dreamed.

God is love. "For God so loved the world, that he gave his only begotten Son, that whosoever believeth on him should not perish, but have everlasting life." John 3:16. God works best through love. He was now ready to move in a way He knew to be most effective at reaching people for eternity.

Heaven's best gift, coming to show the totality of God's love, began by forming a small fellowship of twelve men.

Of course Christ wanted to touch the lives of as great a multitude of people as possible. He had a whole world to win. But even with so much at stake He chose to focus His effort primarily on making God's love real to a few.

Jesus understood that the credibility of His divinity and thus the success of His entire mission on behalf of everyone in the world hinged on His success at helping His disciples to relate to God and to one another in new dimensions of fellowship as loving, caring persons.

Just before His death, Jesus pleaded with the Father in prayer, expressing His longing for the sort of unity, oneness, and closeness He longed to see in His followers. He saw this as the ultimate proof to the world that God had come to the world as a man and had lived His love totally and unforgettably for the saving of the human family. "That they all may be one," Christ prayed, "as thou, Father, art in me, and I in thee, that they also may be one in us: that the world may believe that thou hast sent me." John 17:21.

The Master knew that people would believe the gospel, that Christianity would make a difference in the world, only as sinners would be attracted to those who were living God's love in an unselfish, united, caring, superhuman fellowship. It was His plan to show God's love through the love He had taught His followers to have for one another. His love unites His followers. And when the world sees that love, the world witnesses the divine relationship.

In the concluding hours of His earthly life, at the first communion table among those in whom He had invested so much of Himself, Jesus highlighted specifically the most distinctive characteristic by which His people would be known in the world: "By this shall all men know that ye are my disciples, if ye have love one to another." John 13:35.

Christ foresaw that this circle of loving fellowship which He had generated among the eleven through the years would expand until it would become a great drawing, compelling demonstration to the world and to the universe that the love of God could actually become permanently embedded in human hearts. This became the moving force in human lives that drew people to Him.

Christ has given us, His followers, the responsibility of demonstrating the reality of their faith and thus the reality of their Saviour by the way they relate to one another.

We need to understand how much Christ cared about the quality of the fellowship that exists in His name. We need to realize that He cared enough about it to invest His all in it. We need to see that He cared enough to risk His claim to divinity and thus the very credibility of the entire concept of Christianity. When we are able to grasp its true importance, we are compelled to ask ourselves this question: To what extent is the sort of fellowship Jesus had in mind a reality in the church today? Is the prayer of the soon-to-be-sacrificed Saviour ("that they all may be one; . . . that the world may believe thou hast sent me") being answered in the lives of Christians in our generation?

It is not. Not enough. The greatest need in the church today is its need for love, for oneness, and for fellowship. The world needs nothing so much today as the demonstration through human beings of Christ's love. All heaven waits for men and women through whom God can reveal this power of Christianity.

Must this kind of fellowship remain largely a dream? When will it become a reality? We know on the authority of the Master Himself that we can experience neither the fullness of spiritual life nor a truly fruitful witness to the world until it does.

The basic, practical question facing us now is this: Can something be done immediately on your part and mine to implement this desperately needed fellowship? Or must we sit back and wait for God to bring it about while we watch?

George Webber in his book *The Congregation in Mission* makes this statement: "No relationship of love can develop unless there are structures in which it can grow." This is a basic principle of human dynamics. It is true whether it applies to the love that exists between two persons or between a person and God or among a number of persons, as in a church. God has given us Christians the responsibility of creating the atmosphere and arranging the structure that will best serve as the vehicle for the Holy Spirit to develop a fellowship of love in our midst. God is responsible for the wine. But we must supply the cup. God will light the fire. But we must respond by supplying the candle.

What then is the best structure for Christian fellowship? "It is my conviction," says Howard Snyder in an article in *Christianity Today,* "that the *koinonia* [fellowship] of the Holy Spirit is most likely to be experienced when Christians meet together informally in small-group fellowships." Lawrence O. Richards, in *A New Face for the Church,* writes: "The natural power of group relationships and the overriding power of the Holy Spirit operating through gifted individuals, frees, transforms, and opens up believers to one another and to God. Renewal in the churches demands renewal in the lives of believers. For this, the church must become 'the Church,' and the small group is the ideal context."—Page 173.

And Keith Miller, in *The Taste of New Wine,* says, "We [in a small group] found that it [Christianity] is not a 'religion' at all, but *real* creative life, life in which we are free to be honest about ourselves and to accept and love each other and Him, because the living Christ is in the midst of us . . . winning us to Himself and to His world. Suddenly we had something real to tell, something 'which we have seen and heard!' Together!" Then in concluding his book Miller writes: "The point is, if you genuinely want lay renewal in your church, I believe you will have to have somewhere in your own experience a living, growing, fellowship of people who are being gently crushed into the wine of new life. This family will be the spiritual home, the true center of Christ's church, into which other people can be brought to be loved and reborn."—Page 115.

We have already seen that Jesus introduced a depth, a quality, a warmth into human fellowship never before seen. He chose to form a *group* of twelve men. He demonstrated unforgettably the inherent power and dynamic potential of Christian groups. Christ taught that this sort of structure has a special quality about it that enables Him to accomplish miracles in our lives. "For where two or three are gathered together in my name, there am I in the midst of them." Matthew 18:20.

Paul expected Christians to become deeply involved with each other and to give each other strength and support in fellowship. "Bear ye one another's burdens, and so fulfill the law of Christ." Galatians 6:2.

He taught the basic principle that just as God uses persons to save other persons, so He wishes to use persons to help their fellow believers to mature and to gain spiritual insight in sanctification by helping them within the structure of loving Christian fellowship. He sensed that the honesty of this fellowship must sometimes prove painful: "Be instant in season, out of season; reprove, rebuke, exhort with all longsuffering and doctrine." 2 Timothy 4:2. "Let the word of Christ dwell in you richly in all wisdom; teaching and admonishing one another." Colossians 3:16.

Throughout the New Testament occur references to Christian groups along with guidelines for what can be accomplished in them and through them. The dynamic power of Christian fellowship groups, perfected by Jesus and emphasized by the apostles, is still real today. It is still God's plan.

The formation of small groups as a basis of Christian effort has come from One who cannot err. In large congregations the members should divide into small groups. There they should work not only for fellow church members, but also for unbelievers. They should keep their bond of union unbroken. They should press together in love and unity. They should encourage one another to advance. In this way they can gain courage and strength.

Christian churches have largely disregarded this divine plan in favor of a more formal, rigid structuring. And this is one of the major reasons that the fellowship of love and oneness is so little seen within the Christian movement today. The lack of such small fellowship groups has caused many, especially among young people, to lose confidence in the church and become disenchanted. Some have become convinced that they will never find in the church the missing power and potential they have hoped to see.

Apart from the sort of group fellowship Jesus introduced to His disciples, we cannot experience the full, powerful, and exciting dimensions of love the Master intended as the identifying mark of His following and as the very power behind the Christian movement. No matter how correct a church's theology, or how functional and active its organization, without this kind of loving fellowship it has nothing.

Fortunately, a new experience is penetrating Christian circles. Men and women who all along have sensed something missing have more and more been finding love and fellowship in small groups meeting together.

A pastor's wife writes: "These groups have been the most thrilling experience of my life as a minister's wife. . . . In each group lives are being changed and made ready for the kingdom, and we praise God for what He has done and is doing. . . .

"Since we must share in order to truly love, it could be that our churches lack love for lack of opportunity to share experiences and burdens. As our hearts grow to include the joys and sorrows of those in our group, in addition to our own family and loved ones, we find that our capacity to love others outside of the group increases. . . . As we speak to one another in the group of God's love, we find it easier to speak of the joy of the Christian way to all those we meet."—*The Ministry,* January, 1970, pp. 20, 21.

When new outbreaks of revival and reformation occur, they seem often to arise out of group fellowships. On the other hand, when the group fellowships diminish or are disregarded, the fires of revival seem to burn low.

John, the disciple who learned firsthand from Jesus the dimensions of Christian love, wrote long ago, "But if we walk in the light, as he is in the light, we have fellowship one with another." 1 John 1:7.

If we are going to live God's love, we must live it together. This fellowship involves something of greater depth than occupying the same padded pew for an hour each week in a formalized service! Our church services continue on in a formal way because it is comfortable and convenient. No one has to get involved or take risks. This is foreign to the Biblical concept of the priesthood of all believers, which envisions every Christian ministering to every other. Rigidness and cold formalism are opposite to fanaticism. But both are satanic delusions.

During the week church members should do their faithful missionary work. Then at church they can relate their experiences. Such a meeting can be as food for the hungry. It can bring new life and fresh vigor. When Christians see the great need of working as Christ worked for other human beings, their joyful reports will be filled with power.

In addition to preaching, the church should give opportunity for those who love God to express their gratitude and adoration. The believers can follow this with prayer and testimony. Anyone should feel welcome to help make the services interesting. Rather than meeting simply as a matter of form, we ought to have

145

interchange of thought, testimonies of daily experiences, and opportunity for thanksgiving. Communing together in Christ in this way will strengthen us for trials and conflicts. We cannot be Christians and at the same time withdraw into ourselves. Each one of us is a part of all humanity. And each one's experience will be largely determined by the experience of his fellow believers. We can receive a hundred times the blessings if we assemble together to worship God in this way. And such fellowshiping together will make us glad. We can have the love of Christ glowing within us. We all look forward to the same heaven as our eternal home. We can share the sweetest and most intelligent fellowship together. Our unity can be the wonder of the earth.

This fellowship with other children of God—this foretaste of heaven-come-down-to-earth—is a gift of loving grace. Our Father wants us to enjoy this refreshing, reforming, redeeming love. He wants us to live it out in our lives. When we fail to seek and to claim this gift, this love experience, we in effect reject it.

Let's not allow it to go unclaimed.

15

LOVE IS ALSO FEELING

"Rejoice with them that do rejoice, and
weep with them that weep." Romans 12:15.

Mrs. Woodrum, 55, was a widow living in Chicago.
Her life ended when she leaped from her twelfth-floor
apartment home.

She smiled and waved at the janitor and then leaped.

The note in her room read as follows: "I cannot stand
one more day of this loneliness. I have no friends. I
receive no mail. No one calls me on the telephone. I
cannot stand it any longer."

Her neighbors said, "We did not know she felt that
way."

Mrs. Woodrum's neighbors illustrate how we
Christians can also fail at loving. To disregard another's
feelings is to disregard that person. We cannot disregard
and love at the same time.

People live on the levels of feeling and emotion. On
this level our hopes, dreams, needs, personalities—our
real selves—are most exposed. And on this level our lives
may touch the lives of others most quickly and most
deeply.

For better or worse.

We humans are creatures of feeling. If a man selected the woman he wanted to have for a wife purely by reason, facts, and logic, he would do well to program himself and several females as completely as possible into a computer and let it select a mate for him.

Most people, however, have a way of defying logic when they fall in love. They are attracted to each other and a feeling develops between them. A person marries because he or she feels deeply that the other is the only one, rather than through examining a checklist of qualifications.

Take away the feeling of enjoyment, challenge, and accomplishment from a person's work and his work becomes drudgery. Take away the feelings from a marriage, and it can be worse than no relationship at all.

A man and a woman can share ideas, beliefs, money, food, and sex with one another and still remain strangers. But by sharing love and by entering into each other's feelings, they make the marriage joyful.

How a person feels can overweigh how he thinks intellectually about another individual. What my wife *thinks* about my IQ, talents, abilities, and physical appearance is not as significant to me as how she feels toward me as her husband. If she has good, warm feelings toward me, my inability to do calculus or to play the piano, or my crooked nose, do not mean much as far as our relationship goes.

How do you decide whom to trust as a best friend? Is it not the person you feel the closest to?

Experts at loving realize that emotions, for better or worse, are the essence of human life. To know someone well, you must know his emotions. Acquaint yourself with someone's mind and you can talk ideas with him. Acquaint yourself with his feelings, and you can know his heart.

In an age which has become expert at communicating ideas, concepts, and beliefs, we desperately need people who communicate on the feeling level—people who are willing to get involved and who understand that in its best dimension feeling is love. We need to feel what others feel and let them know in the most effective and appropriate way possible.

"Rejoice with them that do rejoice, and weep with them that weep," the Word commands. Romans 12:15.

Jesus did. He identified with the feelings of others. "For we have not an high priest which cannot be touched with the feelings of our infirmities." Hebrews 4:15.

Jesus revealed love, mercy, and compassion in every act of His life. His heart always sympathized with humanity. He took on our human nature in order to meet our needs. Poor and humble people didn't fear to come near Him. His love attracted little children. They loved to climb upon His lap and gaze into His kind, patient, thoughtful, loving face.

He suppressed no word of truth. But He always spoke in love, tactfulness, thoughtfulness, and kind attention. He was never rude. He never spoke a painful rebuke without absolute necessity. He denied himself. He thought always of others. Every person was precious to Him. He ever bore Himself with divine dignity. But He also bowed with the tenderest regard to every member of the human family.

If you and I imitate Jesus by loving people in depth,

we will be led into a ministry of sympathy and feeling. We should go to our fellow human beings touched as was Jesus, our own High Priest, with the feeling of their infirmities. This does not require us to lose our identities. It does require us to adapt ourselves to the feelings of others.

We must put ourselves in the place of others. We must enter into their feelings, take on their difficulties, disappointments, joys, and sorrows. Closeness and friendship come quickly and spontaneously when, on the feeling level, people share with people. This experience can create the kind of relationship where the truths of the gospel can be communicated most effectively.

Lives cannot be changed by intellectual indoctrination, no matter how skilled the indoctrinator is or how correct his doctrine. Lives are changed only by love. The hungering soul can sense love's reality soonest and best when he sees that you and I care enough about him to be aware of that which is most important. If we want to transform humanity, we must understand humanity. And only through sympathy, faith, and love can we do this. Only in this way can we reach and uplift others.

The foundation of love, as we have seen, is doing or saying what is the best good for another person, regardless of how we feel about them. Yet often the most effective way of doing or saying that which is for another's best good is feeling their sorrows and joys with them and for them. For this reason we need to depend totally on God for success in living God's love.

Christianity involves revealing the tenderest affection for each other. Love is not real unless it is revealed or expressed. As a Christian, commanded to love, I am under obligation to God to learn how to express my affection to people in the most effective ways possible and only for their best good. Jesus identified with the feelings of others and sympathized with them. He has shown us the way.

Yet it is costly to love; it demands total, genuine involvement with other people. Often I don't feel like doing it. By nature I seek involvement with others only for supplying my own emotional or physical needs—not for ministering to theirs. This principle of loving, then, is foreign to what I naturally choose to do.

We love things and use people, the adage goes, when we should use things and love people. Caring about how others feel, expressing concern and interest in them as persons, makes it impossible for me to use them or to treat them as objects!

Our natural concern about other people is usually how they make us feel. Jesus turned this upside down. He showed us that to be an expert at living God's love we must concern ourselves primarily with the way we make other persons feel.

That can be difficult. Especially when we naturally prefer to talk about how we feel—or when others are feeling something uncomfortable, something we would rather not feel. If another feels like weeping, while we feel like laughing, we naturally find it difficult to "weep with them that weep."

Everyone by nature wants freedom to "do his own thing," to become no more involved with others than is convenient. Yet the Bible teaches us as Christians to "look not every man on his own things, but every man also on the things of others." Phillippians 2:4. It also says, "None of us liveth to himself, and no man dieth to himself." Romans 14:7.

God created us people to depend on each other. We need each other physically, spiritually, and emotionally. "Woe to him who is alone when he falls," the Word says, "and has not another to lift him up." Ecclesiastes 4:10, RSV. God lets us know He expects us to get close to other people: "Be kindly affectioned one to another with brotherly love." Romans 12:10.

Christ taught that His spiritual family is to be closer than blood relatives. "And he answered them, saying, Who is my mother, or my brethren? And he looked round about on them which sat about him, and said, Behold my mother and my brethren! For whosoever shall do the will of God, the same is my brother and my sister, and my mother." Mark 3:33-35.

As Christians we all belong to one family; we are all children of the same heavenly Father with the same blessed hope of immortality. The tie that binds us together should be very close and tender. We should come in close touch with those we need to help.

I find many people that I naturally would not prefer to get close to—even in the church. My natural inclination tells me to keep them at an emotional arm's length. I naturally feel that if people outside the church want to get close enough to my ideas and beliefs to qualify to join my church, I have no objection. Any further involvement, however, my nature finds unappealing. But Christ has come to change our natural inclinations!

Let's face it. Some of these people repel us. What would happen to me if I became too involved with someone with unhealthy emotions? Or someone who embarrasses me? What would I do if this person developed a false dependency on me? What would I do if I got so close to people inside or outside the church that they saw me as I really am and realized that I am not everything they now think I am? Or that I want them to think I am?

Someone has termed our time an "emotional ice age." We attach virtue to aloofness. Even in the church, we laud the person who is able to stay unemotional and detached through just about everything.

A person who cannot feel, who is unaware of his own feelings or those of others, is not really alive. "The ennobling difference between one man and another," John Ruskin wrote a hundred years ago, "is that one feels more than another."

Recognizing how people feel and letting them know you know is in practical terms one of the best secrets for living God's love.

To the extent that you and I communicate our awareness of someone's feelings, we succeed at loving him. To the extent that we fail to express our awareness sympathetically, to that extent we fail.

For me it was the beginning of what promised to be a happy day. The sky seemed especially blue. The songs of the birds pleasantly attracted my attention more than usual. I walked briskly toward the hospital.

Everything was going well. My wife had given birth to a baby boy a few days before. We were preparing to leave on a much-looked-forward-to vacation trip to introduce him to his excited grandparents. Life was good.

Checking over the roster of patients on the floor

where I was assigned as a chaplain, I noticed the name of a new admission since my visits the day before. The patient was a female, the card said, about my own age. She was also a registered nurse, as was my wife, and a member of my denomination. Assuming that someone as young as she would not have been admitted for any serious illness and looking forward to a pleasant chat with a person with whom I evidently had much in common, I entered her room.

When I introduced myself to the new patient as the chaplain, the attractive girl greeted me with a friendly smile. She was sitting in a chair in a sunlit corner of her hospital room reading a book. Her tanned face and relaxed manner seemed to confirm my assumption that her medical problems were minor. We quickly fell into conversation. We discussed some of the features of the hospital and joked about the damage her ego might suffer from being "nursed" by other nurses.

After we had chatted for a while the girl went quiet. Then, looking straight at me, she said, "Perhaps you are wondering why I was admitted. I have cancer. It had gone too far before it was discovered. The doctors are doing everything they can to slow it down. But they have told me it is only a matter of time."

I was stunned and repulsed. I did not want to think of something so unpleasant as a charming and attractive person facing imminent death.

This patient had trusted me enough to share with me her overwhelming burden. She had told me plainly about something which was to her an ultimate concern, something about which she had the deepest feelings. How would I react? What would I say?

My response still haunts me. After an awkward pause I stammered, "Oh—uh—I see—"

Then, after another excruciating silence I said, "Uh—I was wondering what school you took your nurses' training at."

She answered my question quickly. After a little more mindless chatter on my part, I left.

How a person could fail more miserably at sympathizing I do not know. Instead of basing my response on her feelings, I had based it on my own. What she had shared distressed me, made me uncomfortable. It did not fit my mood. It was unpleasant. I shrank. I could not accept the challenge or get involved. So I ignored it.

I ignored one of God's children in her hour of greatest need. I cut off any chance of ministering.

What could I have said? The exact words are unimportant. I should have met her at the point of her terrible concern. This is the key to establishing all the relationships we have.

Since love involves awareness of another's feelings, I should have shown her that I at least recognized her feelings. I should have let her know that I knew by appropriately expressing an awareness of her feelings back to her.

Instead of thinking only of myself, my own discomfort, I should have put her first. I should have realized through identification that anyone in such circumstances must have a great deal of anxiety not only for themselves but also for those they love.

I should have said something that would have opened the way for communication between us instead of closing it off. At least she would have understood that I was trying to be aware of how she felt. She would have sensed that I was apparently willing to help her bear her terrible burden. We could have discussed together the things most on her heart. When her confidence in me had been established, I could have offered her reassurance from the Word and helped her to lean on His unfailing love.

But because I did not live His love that day, my chance was almost lost. However, after several days of return visits she finally trusted me enough to share some of the things most important to her.

Letting people's real feelings come through to us and acknowledging our awareness of them by showing that we feel with them and for them is in most circumstances the best and most practical way of expressing love.

A minister once had to carry tragic news to the mother and father of a twelve-year-old boy: Their son had drowned on a school outing. In talking about it later the parents said, "Pastor Barnes didn't preach or read us a Bible text or tell us to be brave. He broke into tears and wept with us. We will always love him for that."

When we as Christians share our feelings with other people, we in reality share the deepest part of our very selves. That is the best gift we can give another person at that point in a relationship. For Christians it means sharing our eternal life in Christ with them. Although it is much easier to give our money, our out-of-style clothes, or even our doctrines, what people really need is deep and open fellowship, the sharing of our affection by the sharing of our feelings.

That costs. It can also be hard work—mentally and emotionally. But in every relationship God is testing us.

He is trying to help us grow and become faithful managers of His love.

Yet, when the Christian strives to become aware of his own feelings and the feelings of others, he does not do so out of narcissistic self-interest or a desire to satisfy curiosity. We must always guard against this. Rather, we must share feelings only from the motive of Christian love. That makes the difference.

A Christian seeks this sort of awareness in order to better understand himself and other people and to develop and mature a relationship, a unity, and a fellowship that could not otherwise exist.

As we have seen, a great principle of human relationships is that, for better or worse, people in fact relate to each other on the feeling level. We share, we communicate best on this level. Awareness of one another's feelings and unity and understanding with them can accomplish the greatest good, invoke the greatest blessings, and communicate the greatest truths.

Jesus recognized this as He worked with His own Twelve. The first disciples exhibited a wide diversity of character and habits. They were destined to be the world's teachers. Jesus knew that to carry forward the gospel successfully these men needed to experience unity of feeling, thought, and action.

By sharing on the feeling level, we Christians can win the confidence of others and consequently open the way to sharing the love and the truth of God with them. Those who can communicate to others their deep feelings for God can introduce men and women to Him in a dynamic way.

One of the best communicators of God's love was the

apostle John. Any Christian who wants to live God's love can profit by studying his life. Through Christ he could relate well on the feeling level. The Bible reveals that Jesus and John developed a deep bond of love. John, the youngest of the Twelve, allowed Christ to open his life so totally that an extraordinary relationship was formed between him and the Master. It was an exceptional relationship, because it existed deeply on the feeling level as well as on all other levels.

Our love for God needs to grow to the point where it exists on a feeling level as well as on the level of the will. What stronger force can exist on earth than the will, the intellect, and feeling united in loving?

John learned from His Lord the importance of communicating on the feeling level. His writings make God's love warm and personal. His epistles breathe a spirit of love as though his pen were dipped in love. Jesus communicated His deepest spiritual teaching through him.

What was John's secret? How could he get so close to Jesus? How could he communicate God's saving truths in a way that would grip hearts? Jesus loves those who really represent the Father. And John could talk of the Father's love as could no other disciple. He revealed to us what he felt in his own soul.

To express God's love sensitively to people on the feeling level as John did can reveal the gospel to the world in a short time! This is why learning truly to live God's love is so important.

We need not feel shame or fear to communicate in this way. Not when we realize that in this way we can love others the deepest, meet their needs the best, and share the eternal truths the most effectively. This is evangelism at its best.

Lack of feeling for people the Bible describes as a symptom of sin in the lives of individuals "who being past feeling have given themselves over unto lasciviousness." Ephesians 4:19. Jesus sounded a similar warning: "And because iniquity shall abound, the love of many shall wax cold." Matthew 24:12. Christ alone can remedy the character defect of indifference.

Paul teaches us to learn in the school of Christ: "And be ye kind one to another, tenderhearted, forgiving one another, even as God for Christ's sake hath forgiven you." Ephesians 4:32.

God wants to develop a group of people today who will allow His divine warmth to penetrate them. This warmth can come only as His love is actively communicated and expressed among people on the feeling level.

"And because iniquity shall abound, the love of many shall wax cold." Coldness is a lack of feeling. It has little to do with the intellect. Human hearts grow cold. Being warmed by God's love and then warming others with it can turn the world upside down again—as it did in the time of the primitive Christian church. We can claim the power of His Word and move forward in faith. You and I can become His experts at the art of Christian loving.

If we will receive the truth of God into our hearts, it will regulate our desires, purify our thoughts, and sweeten our dispositions. It will enliven the faculties of our minds and energize our souls. It will enlarge our capacity for feeling and for loving.

Loving means feeling, and God is waiting for us to start living His love.

The world needs nothing as much as our demonstrations of Christ's love. God waits for us to yield to the influence of His Spirit and thus to reveal Christianity.

"For this is the message that ye heard from the beginning, that we should love one another." "If we love one another, God dwelleth in us, and his love is perfected in us." 1 John 3:11; 4:12.